The High School
PRINCIPAL'S
CALENDAR

To our families—for their love and support

To our students—our hope for the future

To our colleagues—who gave us the gift of their professional practices

THE HIGH SCHOOL
PRINCIPAL'S CALENDAR

A MONTH-BY-MONTH PLANNER
for the School Year

ROBERT RICKEN · RICHARD SIMON · MICHAEL TERC

CORWIN PRESS, INC.
A Sage Publications Company
Thousand Oaks, California

For information:

CORWIN
PRESS

Corwin Press, Inc.
A Sage Publications Company
2455 Teller Road
Thousand Oaks, California 91320
E-mail: order@corwinpress.com

Sage Publications Ltd.
6 Bonhill Street
London EC2A 4PU
United Kingdom

Sage Publications India Pvt. Ltd.
M-32 Market
Greater Kailash I
New Delhi 110 048 India

Printed in the United States of America

Library of Congress Cataloging-in-Publication Data

Ricken, Robert.
    The high school principal's calendar : A month-by-month planner for
the school year / by Robert Ricken, Richard Simon, and Michael Terc.
      p.   cm.
   ISBN 0-7619-7654-X (cloth : alk. paper)
   ISBN 0-7619-7655-8 (pbk. : alk. paper)
   1. Schedules, School—United States—Handbooks, manuals, etc. 2. High
school principals—United States—Handbooks, manuals, etc. I. Simon,
Richard. II. Terc, Michael. III. Title.
LB3032 .R53 2000
373.12'012—dc21

                                       00-009208

This book is printed on acid-free paper.

00 01 02 03 04 05 10 9 8 7 6 5 4 3 2 1

Corwin Editorial Assistant: Kylee Liegl
Production Editor: Denise Santoyo
Editorial Assistant: Cindy Bear
Typesetter/Designer: Marion Warren

Contents

Preface

$\mathcal{F}$or those of you on the front lines, this calendar is the gift of our collective experiences. It is our objective in this book to eliminate as many problems as can be avoided by conscientious planning. In education, our yearly schedule is repetitive inasmuch as annual events and activities recur. Principals must consider holidays as they plan for the year, because these events offer an opportunity to enhance learning and celebrate our common heritage. We include many of the items in our personal "tickler files" here because, properly scheduled, they institutionalize the calm academic environment we strive to create. As administrators, we believe that our main function is to eliminate the distractions that interfere with the tone of our classrooms and student learning, while providing for activities that allow a school to have a character and a heart.

This calendar is intended to be a living document. We have contributed our input, but every item is incomplete because it lacks your interpretation and adaptation to your own school. Our calendar is a series of suggestions to be accepted, modified, or rejected by each building administrator; the value of the text is to stimulate the thinking and planning expertise of each practitioner. We have described practices that have been successful in our schools, but we are aware that these ideas may not be meaningful in your building. The blank lines under each activity will allow you to enter your activities for the month and become our coauthors.

Experienced administrators will be aware that a host of our reminders are familiar. Looking over our calendar should be akin to having a flashback, but we feel the gentle nudge by three colleagues will be appreciated. Students studying to be building administrators are often overwhelmed by the complexity and depth of the planning required by our profession. Each of our suggestions is substantive enough to act as a lesson for the aspiring principal. We firmly believe that the most difficult job in education is that of the high school principal. Issues such as security, drug abuse, teen pregnancy, AIDS, sexism, and state and national standards were of little concern a few decades ago, but are now a major consideration. Principals have an awesome responsibility in an era characterized by the diminution of authority and the increase of student rights. Our aim is that this book will assist you in the same manner as would an informed collaborative colleague.

Experience provides us with the ability to anticipate. We are pleased to share these practices with you. We hope that you add many ideas to your repertoire, and we invite you to send examples of your own practices to us to include them in our next edition.

Acknowledgments

Corwin Press would like to acknowledge the following reviewers:

Steven Ball
Tyner Academy
Chattanooga, TN

Frank Buck
Graham School
Talladega, AL

Paul G. Preuss
Herkeimer BOCES
Herkeimer, NY

Donna Trevathan
Warren County Middle School
McMinnville, TN

Joseph A. Waler
Trinity High School
Garfield Heights, OH

Their contributions are gratefully recognized.

ROBERT RICKEN
RICHARD SIMON
MICHAEL TERC

About the Authors

Robert Ricken, EdD, served as a Junior High School principal and school superintendent in the Mineola School District, and has been an interim superintendent in New York's North Bellmore, Smithtown, Elmont, and Bellmore-Merrick Central high school districts. He was the Long Island Coordinator for the Anti-Defamation League's *A World of Difference Institute*, and conducted antibias workshops and in-service programs in over 100 school districts. He presently teaches educational administration at Long Island University, C. W. Post campus. He is the author of *Love Me When I'm Most Unlovable . . . The Middle School Years, Book Two: The Kids' View, The RA Guide to Nassau County Schools*, and *Middle School Calendar: A Handbook for Practitioners*. He has published articles in *The New York Times, Newsday, Sports Illustrated, The Harvard Review, Harper's Weekly*, and *Single Parent Magazine*. He has also published articles in *The National Association of Secondary School Principals' Journal, The School Administrator, Long Island Magazine, New York State School Board Journal*, and many other professional magazines. He has been designated the Administrator of the Year by Phi Delta Kappa of Hofstra University, the Administrator of the Year by the Nassau-Suffolk Educators' Association, and has been recognized for his work in labor relations by the New York State Council of Administrators and Supervisors. He received the Award of Honor for his outstanding contributions to education through his exemplary public relations practices from the National Public Relations Association. In 1992, he received the Outstanding Service Support Award from the Girl Scouts of Nassau County, and in 1994 received the Dr. Martin Luther King, Jr., Recognition Award.

Richard Simon, MeD, is principal of The Wheatley School, an 8-12 public high school located in Old Westbury, New York. He has served as principal of high schools in New Jersey, Connecticut, and New York. In his 25-year career, he has also taught social studies, advised the student newspaper, and coached a variety of athletic teams and the mock trial team. Mr. Simon received a Geraldine R. Dodge Foundation Fellow for School Leadership Award in 1992, and was named a Council for Basic Education (CBE) Fellow for Independent Study in the Humanities. He received his BA with Phi Beta Kappa honors from Washington University in St. Louis, and his MeD from Harvard University.

Michael Terc, MA, PD, is an administrator in the Mineola public school district. For the past 15 years, he has served as assistant principal at Mineola High School, New York. Before this, he taught mathematics at Mineola Middle School for 16 years. He has also served as principal of the Mineola Summer School Program for two years. During his career, he has coached many sports and has been involved in a host of student activities. He served as president of the Nassau County Baseball Coaches Association and in 1976 was selected as the *Daily News'* High School Baseball Coach of the Year. In 1982, he authored "Coordinate Geometry and Art: A Match," published in *National Council of Mathematics Teachers Journal.* In 1994, he received the Jenkins Service Award, the highest service award given by the Mineola school district's PTA Association. He received his MA in mathematics from Hofstra University, and was awarded a Professional Diploma in educational administration from Long Island University, C. W. Post campus. He recently was selected by the School Administrators Association of New York State to receive its 1999-2000 New York State Distinguished Assistant Principal of the Year Award.

Chapter One

The great leader is he who the people say, we did it ourselves.
Lao-Tsu

*O*nly an experienced school administrator fully understands that the beginning of July is akin to New Year's Eve. It is the time to assess the past year and to utilize our professional creativity to determine the goals for the future. Many of our decisions will be based on the performance quality of the previous year's administrators, teachers, and students.

Optimum planning involves more than assessing the past; doing that is a minimal expectation. The truly effective principal must be a visionary, and in July his or her focus should be directed toward developing strategic future plans.

In the present era of shared decision making, the entire staff should be involved in the planning process. We believe staff members do not maintain a constant level of excellence unless there is a collective vision for the future. That future goal, simply put, is a higher level of performance and a greater commitment to children and our profession. Joint planning and high expectations should be the aura of the high school.

Many of these lofty ideals can be accomplished only if the principal establishes a truly businesslike tone for the school. Phase one of any plan is to create an atmosphere for success. The staff will become believers if they observe daily evidence of the principal's leadership skills. The nitty-gritty things that we do make our faculty become believers. This month's calendar items set the tone for the year ahead, even though the implementation will not become operational until September.

The joy and satisfaction of the end of one year are often replaced by the sudden silence, tranquillity, and loneliness of an empty building. July's struggle is to change gears. The lethargy has to be reversed and replaced by a renewal of energy. Vacation time or a conference may help the principal to make this adjustment.

July Key Tasks

JULY

* *Monitor Summer School*

Summer school is in session, and working relationships with the summer school principal will assume the following items:

1. Rules for behavior are firmly established.

2. Respect for the building is part of the summer school orientation.

3. Pass or fail results are forwarded to the high school promptly in order for schedule changes to be completed prior to the start of the regular school year.

Additional Notes: _____

_____

* *Review Curriculum-Writing Projects*

Many districts pay faculty to revise or create curriculum over the summer. These projects should be supervised by a high school administrator, preferably the chair of the appropriate department. The role of this administrator is to ensure that the staff is performing the tasks outlined in the curriculum-writing proposal. Many finished projects do not reach the faculty in a timely fashion because time to produce the final written and duplicated drafts is not built into the proposal.

Additional Notes: _____

_____

✱ *Review Teacher Evaluations*

The hectic pace of the school year usually makes it impossible for the principal to review the folders of the entire staff. Summer is often used to target several teachers whose performance needs improvement or who are new to the building or profession. Assistant principals and chairpersons, along with the principal, are usually responsible for evaluating the entire faculty. The summer lull is an appropriate time to read each staff folder and to prepare input for your administrative team.

Every teacher should have some specific goals for the upcoming year. Often, we neglect the experienced teacher. They, too, need a "pat on the back," perhaps in the form of a personal note, as well as opportunities to share their expertise. Monitoring new staff members, teaching model lessons, and joining curriculum-writing teams are appropriate tasks in which to involve experienced teachers.

We believe that part of the June final evaluation should be the setting of some goals for the upcoming September. Supervision should be an ongoing process.

Additional Notes: _____

_____

✱ *Meet With Custodial Staff*

Meeting with the head custodian and the supervisor of buildings and grounds is a must. We believe that every one of their staff members should be evaluated, as is done with the professional staff. When custodians are less than effective, the entire building suffers. They are part of the team and should view themselves as members of the high school staff.

Also important is a thorough review of the summer custodial work schedule. New budgets often target building projects, and the principal should set the work priorities with the buildings and grounds administrators. Special projects that were funded in the budget, if completed effectively, demonstrate to board members and staff that the budget-building process is worth the time, energy, and effort.

Additional Notes: _____

_____

✱ *Review and Revise Student Handbook*

With computers, the process of revising the student handbook is more manageable than before. Most administrators maintain files on almost everything they do during the year. An assistant principal in a New York school district informed us that she drops little notes into a file titled *Student Handbook*, noting revisions or ideas for the upcoming year. In July, she reviews each new idea with the principal, and later reproduces the revised handbook.

In one year, she included a wording change in the school's mission statement; a board policy statement in regard to the disciplinary code; a change in assigned locker numbers; an updated list of clubs, advisors, and new staff members; and new requirements for the honor society.

Additional Notes: _____

_____

✳ *Review and Revise Teacher Handbook*

We believe the involvement of a small group of teachers in the process of reviewing and revising the faculty handbook is essential. It is an excellent activity for one or two of our superior staff members: Who better than they should know what teachers need in a handbook? Ideally, the principal (or the principal's designee) merely has to implement their suggestions during the summer. As part of its orientation program, a district in Texas has new teachers evaluate the handbook anonymously. In this way, the principal secures input from new faculty members who often have experience from other settings. (See Resource A—Teachers' Manual Revisions Memo, and Resource B—Teachers' Manual Index.)

Additional Notes: _____

_____

✳ *Review School Board's Policy Manual*

The task of reviewing board policies is easily overlooked during the academic year. The principal should review both building and board policies, with special attention given to new or revised policies. The effect of such changes as new graduation requirements, smoke-free environments, new curricula, and changes in the disciplinary code is a matter that may require a meeting with the school superintendent.

Additional Notes: _____

_____

✳ *Review and Revise Administrative Responsibilities*

We all, at times, get married to tradition, become accustomed to doing things one way; however, we must remember that changes sometimes need to be made. The superintendent of schools has a table of organization for the district;

the principal should have one for the high school supervisory staff. A thorough analysis of the staff and line responsibilities of each administrator ensures that every person and subject area is being appropriately supervised. Shifts in responsibility can be made to improve supervision, to adjust workloads, or to conform to state mandates and laws. With frequent budget shortfalls, the principal would be wise to plan for a reduction in staff and how it would have the least effect on the building's table of organization.

Additional Notes: _____

_____

✳ *Attend Monthly Board Meetings*

Board of education meetings are the high school principal's opportunity to review publicly the achievements of students and staff. It is important for the principal, having just attended all of the closing events and the graduation exercises, to transfer that joy and enthusiasm to the board and community. Sharing news about school achievements in person at board meetings is an incredible public relations opportunity, and subsequently publishing that report in the local newspaper and school district newsletter is vital to securing community support for the high school. We view these activities as a critical segment of a principal's public relations plan.

Additional Notes: _____

_____

✳ *Seek Accreditation*

Any means employed to secure positive acknowledgments of the high school's excellence from outside accrediting agencies is both appropriate and valuable. Their stamp of approval validates every positive aspect of what the high school staff has been articulating to the community. Since criteria differ nationally, we recommend that you apply to your own state or to such organizations as the College Board for accreditation. State and national Schools of Excellence contests, with the potential to bring a prestigious honor to your school district, are also helpful incentives in improving the school's program and staff. These efforts are most successful when the staff buys into the process, as opposed to a "top down" mandate from the administration.

Additional Notes: _____

_____

* *Analyze Trends in Disciplinary Referrals*

Disciplinary trends should be monitored throughout the year, but an annual study is necessary to assess fully the schoolwide program. We suggest that principals perform the following tasks:

1. Compare current numbers of referrals with those from the previous year.

2. Put referrals into categories: misbehavior in class, cutting classes, smoking, fighting, and so forth.

3. Itemize the referrals by teacher.

4. Itemize the referrals by department.

The building principal should hold a July roundtable with the dean or assistant principal in charge of discipline to discuss the data. Significant data should be reviewed and, if necessary, procedures adjusted. Sometimes, individual teachers are submitting an extraordinary amount of referrals, and the principal should alert the appropriate supervisor to assist the staff member with improving classroom management.

Additional Notes: _____

_____

* *Examine School Statistics*

Data, such as the number of students graduating, going on to college, joining the work force, and dropping out of school, should be examined. Final exams and year-end grades should be reviewed by courses, teacher, and department. Significant changes and trends should be reflected in schoolwide and department goals for the upcoming school year.

Additional Notes: _____

_____

* *Assess Each Department*

A meeting should be held with each subject area supervisor to review curriculum changes, personnel issues, and goals for the coming year. This session usually flags potential problems for the chairperson to address.

Additional Notes: _____

_____

✳ *Meet With Parents*

We believe in the ongoing value of meetings between the high school principal and the parents of high school students. These informal, but regular, contacts with parents are an essential and useful activity. The principal can also invite other members of the staff to these meetings to discuss a host of topics that keep parents informed about high school activities, course requirements, and guidance functions. These meetings frequently defuse potential controversial issues. They also afford the principal a pipeline to community feelings about the school's activities and staff.

Additional Notes: _____

_____

✳ *Review District Calendar*

The high school principal should review the school's district calendar for the upcoming academic year. Only those dates that are exclusively high school priorities should be included in the district calendar. Events such as the PSAT, the SAT, graduation, and the school play are a few examples of pertinent items whose dates should be included on the calendar.

The high school calendar must be coordinated by an assistant who has the highest organizational skills and is detail oriented. The plethora of events at any high school should not conflict with other school activities. Special care should be taken to avoid scheduling activities on religious holidays. The skills needed to perform this task are akin to those of the person who develops the master schedule. You simply cannot publish a calendar and then realize that you have conflicts. Scheduling two events at the same time or scheduling an activity that interrupts the educational program causes the staff and community to lose confidence in its management team. Use the past year as a guide, but be certain that requests for changes do not have a negative effect on another club or event. This is one of the rare times when a degree of rigidity is a virtue.

Additional Notes: _____

_____

July Communications

✳ Letter to Staff

We believe that the high school principal should write a letter of thanks to the faculty for their work during the past school year. The principal should include the highlights he or she mentioned in the presentation to the board of education. The letter should be a source of pride for the staff, especially when many faculty and student achievements are noted.

Including some information about the summer curriculum projects demonstrates that, even during the vacation period, the high school is a work in progress. An update on construction projects, painting, and new equipment will also be appreciated.

The next correspondence will probably be the welcome-back-to-school letter. As the summer begins, however, the staff deserves accolades for their past performance and the principal's best wishes.

Additional Notes: _____

_____

✳ Letter to Incoming Class

A letter of welcome is the principal's way of reaching out to the freshman class. This letter is a necessary early notification that serves many institutional, as well as student, needs. Most new students have a high degree of anxiety as they await the start of high school; this letter lets the new ninth graders know that you are preparing for their arrival and want to make their transition as comfortable as possible. It is equally important to include transfer students in this mailing, because they often have the additional fear of being forgotten or overlooked.

This letter should set forth the orientation dates and arrival times. To ensure a smooth school opening, the principal should mention the availability of counselors for August scheduling changes: Any procedure that diminishes scheduling changes is a model administrative practice.

Additional Notes: _____

_____

✳ Letter to New Staff

We should not wait for the end of August to welcome our new staff and begin their orientation program. Many principals invite new teachers in during the summer for an informal chat and to pick up textbooks, curriculum guides, and faculty handbooks. It is a personal touch and a thoughtful way to reach out to new personnel.

This letter usually outlines the orientation process. Some districts not only bring in new teachers early, but also have additional orientation and in-service sessions throughout the school year. In many districts, a business official hosts a meeting to discuss payroll dates, health insurance, social security, and payroll deductions. In addition, union officials may be invited in to discuss the teacher contract; this activity, however, is usually separate from the formal district orientation.

Most of all, the letter is an invitation to the new staff member to join the family and the profession. Many schools assign a new teacher to a mentor, and let new staff know that they will have a confidante when the orientation process is fully operational. A compassionate letter with a hearty welcome is the first phase of a new teacher's orientation process.

Additional Notes: _____

_____

* Contact Local Police and Fire Officials

Every school should have current disaster plans in the event of an emergency. Unfortunately, in contemporary America, violence, bomb threats, fire, and civil disturbances are a possibility and should be anticipated. Because school laws and local statutes change frequently, the principal should learn, in consultation with local law enforcement officers and school attorneys, his or her rights and responsibilities on a yearly basis. For example, in New York State, the principal may resume classes after searching a building during a bomb scare; however, once the building is emptied and police are called in, the students may not reenter without police—not the school principal's—approval. Good relations are helpful during these troubled and uncertain emergency situations. In this catch-22 environment, caution is the word. Police professionalism should be respected, but the principal's duty to act *in loco parentis* is of paramount importance. The students are, in the final analysis, our children.

Fire officials should be given equal time. Most state education departments require a specific number of fire drills a year; most insist upon a dozen drills, with approximately eight performed prior to December 31. Fire officials may check alarm boxes and discuss response time in emergency situations. Principals should be aware that, in a fire, the number of casualties increases dramatically if students take longer than two minutes to exit a building.

Such meetings with police and fire officials foster good relations with two of the community's most important service organizations. In most rural and suburban districts, the fire personnel are usually volunteers, and often your students' older siblings and parents.

Additional Notes: _____

_____

✳ *Membership in Civic Associations*

Principals should consider joining groups such as the Rotary Club, the Lions, the Kiwanis, and the local Chamber of Commerce. The benefits are obvious. Membership provides support for high school activities, and principals are in turn able to present information about their students and staff to members of these prestigious organizations. Joining all clubs is not always practical; thus, the decision should be evaluated annually.

One possible strategy is to encourage assistant principals to join other local organizations to increase the school's involvement in such public relations efforts. The members of these service organizations are key communicators in the community. The principal's membership to such groups often translates into a positive information flow to his or her residents.

Additional Notes: _____

_____

✳ *Subscribe to Local Newspapers*

Being aware of local politics and community developments is vital to your job as principal. Civic newsletters and the letters to the editor section of the local paper provide a rich source of information. In addition, sending news releases on awards, honor roll lists, and school activities is another way to inform your public about the school. This two-way flow of information benefits everyone. We have found, by the way, that local newspapers provide more thorough high school coverage than do the major newspapers.

Additional Notes: _____

_____

✳ *Develop a Public Relations Program*

A written public relations program has all of the desired outcomes we have mentioned in the previous two tasks. Some districts have developed rather sophisticated public relations programs. A principal from Indiana, for example, sent us the following list of one-line PR ideas when responding to our query about his program:

1. School Awards Night

2. Student handbook, book covers, and a book of course offerings

3. Senior-to-Senior (citizen) Day

4. High school bulletin boards

5. Letters to parents

6. Awards assembly for athletes and participants in extra-curricular activities

7. Honor Society induction ceremony

8. Music concerts

9. Drama performances

10. School newspaper

11. PTA meetings

12. Board of education presentation

13. College and Career Nights

Public relations, as you can see, is a broad-based, multifaceted approach to building community understanding and support for the complete array of activities going on within the high school. More is better!

Additional Notes: _____

_____

July Planning

* *Summer Administrative Team Workshop*

Every activity we have discussed so far is a potential agenda item for a summer workshop. Most principals give their administrative staff an opportunity to submit items for such a meeting. Putting the items of the workshop agenda in priority order maximizes the outcome. This is a time to focus on schoolwide concerns, to consider strategies to improve the effectiveness of the entire high school, and to set specific future priorities.

Additional Notes: _____

_____

* *Plan Field Trips and Fundraising Activities*

Our purpose in this book is to help principals develop a conflict-free calendar. Annual trips taken by performing groups, such as the marching band, should not be planned when their services are required at community parades or athletic contests. As the number of school activities expands, conflicts even arise during the summer. A principal in Wisconsin mentioned his dilemma when the summer football camp was scheduled during the same week in August as the music and drama groups held their annual tryouts. There were not only students who wanted to be involved in both activities, but there were faculty disputes over the use of the grounds and facilities.

In terms of organizing fundraising events, one assistant principal in Mineola, New York, created a fundraising schedule to avoid misunderstandings between school groups over the sale dates and the specific items to be marketed. What was once a cause of discontent is now a mutually agreed upon standardized practice. (See Resource C—Meetings Calendar Memo, and Resource D—Fundraising Calendar Memo.)

Additional Notes: _____

_____

✳ *Student Orientation*

An orientation program for new students should be planned at this time to ensure such students a comfortable start to the school year.

Additional Notes: _____

_____

July Personnel

✳ *Staffing and Tenure*

All faculty positions and schedules should be monitored and finalized at this time. Any openings should be posted and advertised, and arrangements should be made for summer interviews. This process should be followed for all support staff as well, with a roster of staff positions being posted.

We believe that all cocurricular positions should also be filled as early as possible, as this contributes to a smooth opening for these activities in September. Coaching assignments should also be made at this time. Ideally, faculty advisors of cocurricular activities will be able to plan for these events over the summer.

A final check should also be made of contractual obligations. Timelines should be followed for staff members who are scheduled for appointment to tenure, and tenure recommendations should be made for the coming year. A similar review should be made for the nonteaching staff, particularly in states where they are governed by civil service law. They, too, have a form of tenure after a brief probationary period.

Additional Notes: _____

_____

July Checklists

July Key Tasks

Major Assignments	Date Started	Date Completed	Days on Task
Monitor summer school			
Review curriculum-writing projects			
Review teacher evaluations			
Meet with custodial staff			
Review and revise the student handbook			
Review and revise the teacher handbook			
Review the school board's policy manual			
Review and revise administrative responsibilities			
Attend monthly board of education meetings			
Seek accreditation of high school			
Analyze trends in disciplinary referrals			
Examine school statistics			
Assess each department's status			
Meet with parents			
Review the district calendar			

July Communications

	Assignment
	Write a letter to the staff
	Write a letter to the incoming freshman class
	Write a letter to new faculty members
	Contact local police and fire department officials
	Establish membership in civic associations
	Subscribe to local newspapers
	Develop a public relations program

July Planning

	Assignment
	Conduct a summer administrative team workshop
	Finalize the new student orientation program
	Finalize the calendar for field trips and fundraising activities

July Personnel

	Assignment
	Finalize faculty positions and teaching schedules
	Finalize rosters for all other staff positions
	Appoint cocurricular advisorships
	Make coaching assignments
	Make tenure recommendations for the next year

JULY CALENDAR

MONTH: JULY

YEAR: _____

MONDAY	TUESDAY	WEDNESDAY	THURSDAY	FRIDAY	SATURDAY / SUNDAY

Notes: _____

Ricken, R., Simon, R., & Terc, M. The High School Principal's Calender. © 2000. Corwin Press, Inc.

Chapter
Two

The school's momentum is fueled by the passion of its principal.
Author Unknown

*A*ugust is the month of transition from summer to the new school year. It signals a return to an action mode. Each item on your to-do list, if properly addressed, will help provide a smooth opening of school. While every state does not begin the school year in September, the ideas and strategies provided here are applicable to all schools.

Processing the information you discovered while meeting with key staff members over the past two months should provide the current data necessary for setting realistic future goals. Now is clearly the time to formulate plans to help provide a clear focus for the coming months. Today, most schools involve the community as well as the staff in this process. School improvement teams and site-based councils help to foster ownership in the school and to mobilize constituent groups to assist in achieving these new goals.

We believe that the principal should establish personal goals as well. This task is left to you; however, when we examine why most principals have difficulty in achieving their own personal agenda, we find that the day-to-day pressures of the job often make self-reflection impossible. How can one look within when one's to-do list is always full? A word about time management is appropriate here, because since using time efficiently ultimately determines how effectively we plan our day and execute our priorities. The National Association of Secondary School Principals (NASSP) Department of Student Activities provides the following valuable tips for managing one's time:[1]

1. Pinpoint the time of day when you are most productive; make the most of it.

2. Eliminate distractions in prime time.

3. Schedule high priority, tough, and ugly jobs for prime hours.

4. Schedule easier, more interesting tasks for off-peak times.

5. Give low priority tasks the least attention.

6. Eliminate unimportant activities.

7. Make decisions now.

8. Make more realistic estimates of the time needed to complete a task.

9. Set priorities among each day's jobs.

10. Break tasks into manageable sections.

11. Set deadlines for each section.

12. Finish tasks before starting new ones.

13. Delegate jobs that can be done by others.

14. Eliminate excessive paperwork.

15. Limit conversations to important items.

16. Pace your work to get results within a reasonable period of time.

17. Schedule breaks or changes in routine to avoid fatigue.

18. Limit your work hours each week.

19. Work while others are at lunch; eat earlier or later than others.

20. Arrive at appointments on time by listing when you have to leave, not the time of the appointment.

21. Have only one project—the one you are currently working on—on your desk at a time.

22. Ask for information when you do not understand or need more facts.

23. Keep communication lines open.

24. Train staff members for new tasks.

25. Anticipate changes; prepare for them.

26. Confine conflicts to issues, not personalities.

Ideally, this list will provide one or two hints that will enable each principal to maximize his or her constructive time.

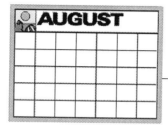

August Key Tasks

* *Prepare School-Opening Remarks for Staff*

We view this "Welcome back" speech as one of the principal's important lesson plans. As with any teacher lesson, all of the component parts should be included. Too many principals talk off-the-cuff and do not focus their remarks. Such an informal greeting even breaks the law in certain states where such items as disciplinary codes and emergency situations must be mentioned.

The scope of this presentation is limitless. Professors of educational administration frequently give their students this final examination question: Write your school-opening speech for the first conference day held just prior to the start of school. In the list below, we provide some critical components to the speech; we are aware, however, that you will delete some and add many of your own as you prepare for the new academic year.

1. Express thanks for your faculty's past efforts.

2. Assert your hope that the well-deserved rest served to renew energy for the new year.

3. Introduce the chairperson or mentor who will introduce new staff members.

4. Review summer projects and accomplishments.

5. Review legal data (if required).
   Example: Remind staff that, in New York State, any mention of child abuse must be reported, whether substantiated or not.

6. Read the building's mission statement as an inspirational theme.

7. Getting started:
   * Review disciplinary code.
   * Highlight some faculty handbook items.
   * Discuss first-day class expectations.

8. Reminders for first homeroom:
   * Distribute student schedules.
   * Distribute locker assignments.
   * Take attendance.
   * Discuss absence notes.

9. Review teacher responsibilities:
   * Define attendance procedures.
   * Discuss lesson plans.
   * Define grading procedures.
   * Explain procedures for signing in and out.
   * Discuss building assignment and duty periods.

Additional Notes: _____

_____

* Meet With Supervisors

Supervisors are key members of your school team. It makes sense, therefore, to secure their input for your opening-day remarks. In the process, you may be able to emphasize items that they will be discussing later with their departments, and they may broaden your perspective and vision about your initial faculty meeting. By discussing with your supervisors how to motivate the entire faculty, you will be demonstrating your expectations for your supervisors.

This meeting is also your last chance to discover if there are any urgent needs at the department or classroom level. Each supervisor should be able to report on the readiness of his or her own department. Obviously, there is an unspoken expectation that they have visited every classroom and talked with all of their classroom teachers.

This is also the appropriate time to review each supervisor's goals, departments, and objectives for individual teachers. Ideally, this will be a review of what was discussed in June, when you closed the books on the previous school year. This process ensures an orderly transition and a coherent supervisory process.

Additional Notes: _____

_____

* Board of Education Presentation

Some districts require a board presentation by each principal prior to the start of school. If this is necessary, you have the perfect opportunity to present the accomplishments of the past and to survey the goals for the coming year. Involving the staff in the preparation of this speech serves as a reminder of the recent progress made by the high school teachers, and is often a major boost to morale.

Additional Notes: _____

_____

❋ *Establish Field Trip Parameters and Cutoff Dates*

Surprise field trips create conflicts between departments. The lab teacher who has spent a great deal of time setting up a special science experiment should not discover suddenly that half of his class is on a field trip. A schedule of field trips should be published, and reminders should appear on the weekly memo to staff several weeks prior to the event. Cutoff dates have become necessary because of final examinations and required testing. High school teachers have a right to be concerned if there are many field trips during the last few weeks of school. For schools that end in June, we recommend that there be no field trips after the first week in May. In other words, we suggest that the administrator set a closing date for class excursions that provides maximum class time for the last six weeks of school.

Additional Notes: _____

_____

❋ *Establish Fire Drill Schedule*

Many states require a specific number of fire drills per year. Some also add to these demands the fact that two thirds of the drills should be held prior to the winter recess, which makes sense, since the procedures should be clear to staff and students alike. The latter part of the fire drill schedule should be flexible, because a break in the winter weather sometimes allows the administrator to hold a surprise fire drill or make up for one that was canceled because of inclement weather.

Additional Notes: _____

_____

August Communications

❋ *Meet With Parent-Teacher Organizations*

Principals should meet with the PTA president or with the entire executive board. The reservation of meeting dates should be established in June to ensure that meetings do not conflict with other school activities. The time, dates, and purpose of the meeting should now be reviewed and finalized. The topic of the meeting should be discussed at this time, and new items that have a degree of urgency can be substituted for less urgent program ideas.

We recommend a hands-on approach for the principal when planning PTA activities. The principal should participate in each meeting; a poor meeting or disgruntled parents ultimately become the principal's problem. Active participation will usually maximize the high school's positive image and avoid the escalation of controversial issues. Your participation and expertise will guarantee a feeling of mutual support and a properly focused agenda.

Additional Notes: _____

_____

✳ *Inspirational Speech*

At times, experienced principals do not make the most of the opportunity afforded by an inspirational speech. Your entire staff deserves to hear your thoughts for the new school year and your appreciation for their past efforts. Since they are refreshed and rejuvenated, we recommend you seize the moment. If the speech is successful, your staff will look forward to the challenge ahead and be proud to be a member of the high school. This is your August meeting assignment. Due date: First day with staff.

Additional Notes: _____

_____

✳ *Submit June Examination Grades and Analysis to Superintendent*

Part of the process of submitting June examination grades and an analysis of them is the need to meet individually with each department leader to discuss the results of final examinations, standardized tests, and state assessments. These items have become more prevalent throughout the nation in this era of accountability; reviewing the results of testing affords us the opportunity to monitor the instructional program. Doing an item analysis might inform us of the fact that we are not teaching a particular topic properly or perhaps that it is not even a part of our curriculum. At the present time, testing and comparing results with other districts is a reality that principals must acknowledge. Furthermore, understanding testing and being able to articulate the results is an additional skill that should be developed if it is not already a part of your expertise.

The superintendent will be very interested in the testing results. He or she will also be accountable, and must therefore be prepared to explain the data to the board of education and to the entire school community. Ideally, testing will remain just one way to evaluate a department or a school's progress.

Additional Notes: _____

_____

❋ *Principal's Newsletter*

We believe that the principal's newsletter serves many valid educational purposes. It is a public relations document for the school year. It serves to increase the morale of both students and staff. It is an opportunity to give accolades for outstanding performance or service to the community. It informs the entire community about the school's progress and the extraordinary efforts of the students and teaching staff. The newsletter should also give the principal a sense of progress, and should assist in setting greater expectations for the remainder of the year. The document should be forwarded to the superintendent, who, ideally, will share your school's achievements with the board of education.

Additional Notes: _____

_____

❋ *Other Communications*

Principals should remember at this time to send out opening-of-school letters: one to faculty and staff, and one to parents and students with parking application and transportation information. In addition, mail schedules and the opening-day program to students. Now is also a good time to write an article for the student newspaper.

Additional Notes: _____

_____

August Planning

❋ *Establish Goals and Projects*

Determining goals and projects should be the result of all your meetings with supervisors, teachers, parents, and students. Their implementation will demonstrate the collective vision of your school community.

Undertaking them also indicates that we believe in the improvement process and resist resting on our past laurels. The principal, like the staff, should establish new priorities each school year. These goals may be short-term or multiyear projects. A good example of a short-term goal might be to measure the number of cuts or discipline cards from last year to the conclusion of the present year to determine if the disciplinary plan is paying dividends. The principal's projects listed below include both short- and long-term goals.

Specifying projects and listing them in priority order should provide attainable objectives that enhance your supervisory model, curriculum, or facility. A principal from Connecticut formulated the following projects recently, and reported that each was completed in a single school year:

1. Revise the health curriculum and secure the approval of the superintendent and board of education.

2. Rewrite the portion of the disciplinary code dealing with lateness to class to reduce the problems perceived by staff.

3. Institute a new site-based management team to address the community's request to revise our local graduation requirements.

4. Establish a student-faculty committee to ensure consistency in the selection of students for extra-curricular activities and to establish an equitable process for excluding students from participation.

5. Complete the following facility improvements:
   * Construct bookshelves in all social studies classrooms.
   * Construct bulletin boards for the Physical Education Department.
   * Add electrical outlets in rooms 212, 214, 305, and all science labs.
   * Construct a small basement area to house records of students who graduated before 1985.
   * Construct shelves in the in-school suspension room, and stock them with the required texts from each department.
   * Remove graffiti, and paint both portable classrooms and all outside storage sheds.
   * Reline all parking spots, and fill in all potholes before spring recess begins.

Additional Notes: _____

_____

* *School-Opening Packet for Staff*

We are certain that in your files, your secretary or assistant principal will be able to obtain last year's informational packet. Ideally, other ideas were added to your files during the first month or two of the previous school opening. Update your staff informational packet, remembering that some topics may be duplicated in the *Teachers' Manual*. Here is a list of items that you might want to include as you develop your own packet:

1. First day of school bell schedule.

2. First homeroom information:
   * Emergency home contact cards.

* Distribution of student schedules.
* Notes for absences.

3. First class session reminders:
   * Discuss curriculum.
   * Discuss discipline.
   * Discuss homework procedures.
   * Distribute books and have students provide a protective cover.
   * Teach a mini-lesson.
   * Discuss class regulations.
   * Point out the location of the in-school detention/suspension room.
   * Discuss attendance procedures for both the homeroom and classes.

4. Duty assignment job descriptions.

5. Date of first fire drill (pre-announced).

6. Reminder that staff check for fire drill signs and know evacuation routes.

7. Review of grading procedures.

Additional Notes: _____

_____

* *Last-Minute Double Checks*

One of the greatest gifts a principal can give to the staff is to guarantee a smooth opening. We make similar demands on teachers, requesting that they be prepared and organized from day one of the school year. A final check of the items listed below is part of a principal's lesson plans or, more accurately, school-opening plans. If these questions are asked, and things are properly inspected and operating, the school should open in an orderly manner.

1. Is PA system working? Is the bell system working?

2. Are all fire extinguishers operable?

3. Are all emergency systems in order? (e.g., Are there exit lights, fireboxes, and emergency exit directions in each room?)

4. Are student lockers cleaned and repaired?

5. Are there flags in each classroom?

6. Are televisions in working order?

Additional Notes: _____

_____

✱ *Final Walk-Through With Head Custodian*

The principal provides an extra set of eyes for assessing the work of the custodial staff. The building may be clean, but the principal's expertise is to find items that may affect the smooth opening of the school or may prove a safety hazard. In one of our walk-throughs, we found the following oversights:

1. Fire exits were not posted.

2. There were no garbage cans in the cafeteria.

3. Stairwell lights were not operating.

4. Three classrooms were missing desks.

5. The P.A. system was not operating in the resource room.

6. Classroom keys were missing for three homeroom teachers.

7. Flags were needed for several classrooms.

8. The gymnasium floor was still sticky from the recent waxing.

These items can be viewed as minor problems, but by addressing them prior to the opening of school, the administrator has done his or her part to guarantee a smooth first day of classes.

Additional Notes: _____

_____

August Personnel

✱ *Complete Master Schedule*

The master schedule includes teaching assignments, departmental supervision, and room assignments. This last task is often given less consideration than the other two. High school teachers who are forced to travel from room to room rarely take pride in the appearance of their learning space. Proximity to the departmental office also assists in teacher supervision and staff effectiveness. Having a departmental wing in the building is an asset to the instructional program and the tone of the building. Less travel time for staff adds to their preparedness and assures us that teachers will be in their classrooms before their students arrive.

Additional Notes: _____

_____

✻ *Establish Shared Decision-Making Committee Meeting Dates*

Many states now require shared decision-making committees. Some are mandated by state law, and others have been negotiated by teachers' unions. Some states now include parents and high school students on these teams. We endorse this form of collective decision making: Every contemporary text on supervision extols the virtues of shared decision making, and the confident principal is not threatened by the input of the teaching staff. Setting the specific dates for these meetings in a high school is critical, because teachers also attend faculty, department, and districtwide committee meetings.

Additional Notes: _____

_____

✻ *Last-Minute Considerations*

Remember to review and update your list of substitute teachers before the beginning of the school year. In addition, you should ensure that the staff directory has been revised.

Additional Notes: _____

_____

August Checklists

August Key Tasks

Major Assignments	Date Started	Date Completed	Days on Task
Prepare school-opening remarks for staff			
Meet with all supervisors			
Give a presentation at the board meeting, if required			
Establish field trip parameters and cutoff dates			
Establish a fire drill schedule for the year			

August Communications

	Assignment
	Meet with PTA leaders
	Prepare and deliver school-opening inspirational speech
	Submit an analysis of June examination and grade results to the superintendent
	Develop a submission and publication schedule for the principal's newsletter
	Send out opening-of-school letters to parents and students with parking application and transportation information
	Mail student schedules and the opening-day program
	Write an article for the student newspaper
	Send out an opening-of-school letter to faculty and staff

August Planning

	Assignment
	Establish goals and projects
	Prepare an opening-of-school packet for faculty
	Conduct planned orientation program for new teachers
	Complete last-minute double checks
	Conduct a final walk-through with the head custodian
	Establish, as part of the opening packet for staff, the first-day activities for faculty, including plans to teach a mini-lesson

August Personnel

	Assignment
	Complete the master schedule and fill remaining faculty and staff positions
	Establish shared decision-making committee meeting dates
	Review and update the substitute teacher list
	Revise the staff directory

Note

1. This list is reprinted with permission from Ricken, R. (1995). *The Middle-Level Calendar.* Reston, VA: NASSP. For more information regarding NASSP services and/or programs, please call (703) 860-0200.

AUGUST CALENDAR

MONTH: AUGUST

YEAR: _____

MONDAY	TUESDAY	WEDNESDAY	THURSDAY	FRIDAY	SATURDAY / SUNDAY

Notes: _____

Ricken, R., Simon, R., & Terc, M. The High School Principal's Calender. © 2000. Corwin Press, Inc.

Chapter Three

*Integrity is not a 90% thing, not a 95% thing;
either you have it or you don't.*
Peter Scotese

A successful school opening is the direct result of the administrative team's summer planning. A calm and orderly opening of school is not the norm, nor is it accidental. The following key tasks take the principal's time and professional expertise, but go a long way toward ensuring a smooth opening day. Although the checklist can be reproduced each year, details of the experience should be noted, and appropriate ideas for updating it should be filed for future reference. One week after the start of school, a principal from Texas asks all staff members to evaluate the opening of school. These suggestions are then placed in his summer file to improve the following year's process.

The long list of September tasks can be quite intimidating. They not only are numerous, but are also open-ended. Furthermore, each item often justifies a host of subtopics. The sheer number of tasks can easily overwhelm the new principal. The experienced administrator understands that certain jobs must be delegated, whereas others are planned cooperatively and some are personal priorities. For each item mentioned, the principal might want to think who should be primarily responsible for coordinating the activity.

September
Key Tasks

SEPTEMBER

* *First Faculty Meeting*

The first faculty meeting sets the tone for the year. Combine the required opening-of-school information with an activity that focuses attention on the mission of the school. Introduce the new staff, review state-mandated topics, highlight the faculty handbook, and review safety procedures. Remember to also make time to share an inspirational story.

Additional Notes: _____

_____

* *Opening Preparations*

Have bus drivers do a "dry run" the day before school opens to avoid late bus arrivals. Bring in cafeteria aides prior to the start of school to increase efficiency of the first day's lunch periods. Cycle the bells for a day to check that they are all functioning properly. Check out the PA system to make sure all rooms are receiving the announcements.

Additional Notes: _____

_____

* *Meet With Security and Supervisory Staff*

Meet with the security staff to review procedures and to discuss their roles and responsibilities. Use role-playing techniques to remind staff of how to handle sensitive and difficult situations. Provide faculty supervisors of detention, study halls, cafeteria, and halls with clear expectations and enforcement procedures; doing so will help to minimize problems and confrontations. (See Resource E—Building Security Memo.)

Additional Notes: _____

_____

* *New Students*

Make it a point to meet new students to the school personally. Build this meeting into the orientation program that the guidance department provides as part of the registration process. Follow up by monitoring the students' transition after the first few weeks of school.

Additional Notes: _____

_____

✻ *New Teachers*

Meet with the new teachers to assist them in learning about the culture and practices of the school. Limit the specifics to only those topics that are necessary for a successful start to the year. Plan a series of follow-up sessions to cover issues that arise later in the year. Use the follow-up sessions as a place to gain feedback about the school and to brainstorm ideas about how to improve the school or solve problems. (See Resource F—Orientation Agenda.)

Additional Notes: _____

_____

✻ *Superintendent Reports*

Remember to complete all required reports for the superintendent. Have your secretary keep a list of due dates, and double-check important data to ensure accuracy.

Additional Notes: _____

_____

✻ *Public Address System*

Meet with all staff members who regularly use the public address system to review expectations, limits, appropriateness of announcements, and so forth. Limit the use of the system as much as possible to minimize class disruptions and to increase the impact of the few announcements that are made outside of the regular time.

Additional Notes: _____

_____

✻ *Cocurricular Advisors*

The cocurricular program of activities and clubs is a very important part of any school. All too often, major controversies develop from a club or activity. To minimize this, meet with all of the advisors to review such things as procedures, philosophy, and financial rules. Develop and distribute a student activities guidebook to help standardize related procedures and responsibilities.

Additional Notes: _____

_____

✳ *Safety Drills*

No area is more important than ensuring the safety of all students and staff. To do so, you should follow all state and local regulations, pre-announce the first fire drill to ensure that it serves as a model for all future drills, check all safety equipment, and consult with the local police, fire, and ambulance officials.

Additional Notes: _____

_____

✳ *Student Spirit*

Use the first few weeks of school to build school spirit. Such events as the first pep rally, assembly, and dance should be well publicized and supported. Make sure that all bulletin boards are decorated, and that the hallways are bright and cheerful.

Additional Notes: _____

_____

✳ *Grant Proposals*

Work with the appropriate central office and building staff to identify and complete all required grant proposals, and take advantage of some of the many optional grants that are also available. Grant funds can serve as a significant supplement to the budget, and can provide funding for those last-minute opportunities for special programs and activities that would otherwise not be affordable.

Additional Notes: _____

_____

✳ *Staff Development*

Have each department create a staff development plan for the year. This plan should be linked to the building and district goals and priorities for the year. These plans will provide a framework for distributing funds and resources for staff development, and for identifying staff to attend appropriate conferences and training programs.

Additional Notes: _____

_____

September Communications

✳ *Memo to Staff*

We recommend that every high school principal produce a weekly memorandum for the staff. The purpose of the memo is to inform everyone about the events of the week, future activities, and due dates. High school faculties are larger than those in other buildings; it is easy, therefore, for a teacher and principal to have limited personal contact during the school day. The weekly memo helps bridge that communication gap. Teachers should be encouraged to submit items, creating a two-way means of communication, and thus making the memo more valuable. (See Resource G—Weekly Memo.)

Additional Notes: _____

_____

✳ *Class Visits*

The administrative team should visit classes to review the student handbook with the students and to emphasize expectations for student behavior. One principal developed a "quiz" on the handbook, and awarded gift certificates to the school store to the student with the best score in each class. These classroom visits also give the administrative team a chance to interact with many of the faculty over the first few days of the school year.

Additional Notes: _____

_____

✳ *Reports on School Opening*

You are the most visible spokesperson for your school, and so it is important that you provide both oral and written reports about the school's opening to the major constituencies you serve. Use the first PTA and board of education meetings of the school year to highlight the opening of the building, focusing on the many positive student and faculty accomplishments completed over the summer and the smooth manner in which instruction began.

Additional Notes: _____

_____

✳ *Open School Night Letter*

A special letter to all parents inviting them to attend the Open School Night is a must. The letter should include the agenda for the evening, a description of expectations, and a reminder to parents that the focus is on the curricular program, not on individual students. Provide refreshments in the cafeteria, and invite your student clubs and organizations to sell their fundraising items and to market the yearbook and school newspaper.

Additional Notes: _____

_____

✳ *Parent Newsletter*

A monthly letter home from the principal is an opportunity to share student and staff awards, as well as to inform parents about the most pressing issues that the school faces. The letter should include a calendar page with a list of student activities. Your PTA should also be encouraged to include flyers and materials as part of the mailing.

Additional Notes: _____

_____

✳ *Special Education*

Both classified and "504" students are entitled to a variety of accommodations. Remember formally to remind faculty of their responsibilities in this area, and to provide them with a list of students in each category, along with the accommodations they should be receiving. This memo should clearly be marked *Confidential* to protect student privacy.

Additional Notes: _____

_____

✳ *National Merit Winners*

Each fall, one or more students will receive status as a National Merit semifinalist or commended student. Use this as an opportunity to recognize not only the student, but the teachers as well. In addition, remember to give credit to the staff at your elementary and middle schools for preparing the students so well. This type of acknowledgment goes a long way toward promoting harmony in the district. Use the press release form provided by the organization, and send it to your local papers along with a photo of the winners.

Additional Notes: _____

_____

✳ *Deficiency Letters*

Work closely with your nurse to give parents ample written notice of any deficiencies in meeting state and local immunization requirements. Such deficiencies are often a problem with transfer students; an early letter and a follow-up call can help make for a smooth transition to a new school.

Additional Notes: _____

_____

✳ *Problem Students*

Meet regularly with the school's Child Study Team (CST) and Pupil Personnel Service (PPS) team to monitor problem students. The issues discussed at these meetings will often give you advanced notice of the trends and issues in the community. Ensure that the team includes the nurse, social workers, the school psychologist, counseling staff, special education teachers, and any other staff on an as-needed basis.

Additional Notes: _____

_____

September Planning

✳ *Assemblies*

Student assemblies are a wonderful opportunity to build school spirit and share important information with the student body. Planning is the key to effective assemblies. Provide a seating chart and clear directions to staff, and a set of behavioral expectations for students. The principal should run the first assembly, and make it a model for the year.

Additional Notes: _____

_____

✳ *Open School Night*

Preparation is the foundation for a successful Open School Night. Invite a student service club to serve as guides for parents, who often do not know their way around the school. Have backup student schedules available for those parents who forget to bring the one that was sent with the invitation letter. Hold a brief assembly to start the evening and remember to introduce your administrative team. You should also ensure that you are available throughout the evening to answer questions and handle any difficult issues that may arise.

Additional Notes: _____

_____

✳ *Meetings Calendar*

Develop and distribute a calendar that lists all the meetings for the month. This calendar will help in finding common time for the many ad hoc and emergency meetings that must be held during the course of a month. The calendar will also help faculty to improve attendance at key meetings, such as the monthly faculty meeting.

Additional Notes: _____

_____

✳ *Guidance Newsletter*

Maintaining regular communication between the school and the home is vitally important. Some type of monthly newsletter should go home, either through the guidance office or through the principal's office. Publish a schedule for the year, and make it clear that staff members are expected to submit items for inclusion. Student and staff awards, reminders, and parenting advice should all be a regular part of the newsletter. Make sure that the PTA and other parent-run organizations have the schedule and are invited to include announcements and flyers.

Additional Notes: _____

_____

✳ *Student Activities Meeting Calendar*

Most high schools have a rich and varied group of student clubs and service organizations. Many groups look for opportunities to raise money through such activities as car washes or bake sales. Coordination of these activities is important to avoid overlap and injured feelings. Spreading out schoolwide programs, such as pep rallies, assemblies, and fundraising activities, reduces disruptions to the academic program. A well-communicated and well-maintained calendar will prevent many problems.

Additional Notes: _____

_____

✳ *Meet-Your-Coaches Night*

Athletics is a major part of most high schools and can present a major drain on the principal's time if managed poorly. Be proactive by holding an annual Meet-Your-Coaches Night. The athletic director should define the term *student athlete,* and all coaches should be available to meet with parents and to discuss their expectations. One high school begins the evening with a video-highlight film of the previous year's teams. Every parent likes the opportunity to see his or her student on the big screen.

Additional Notes: _____

_____

✳ *Faculty Inservice Sessions*

Each state requires a variety of annual training or inservice sessions for faculty. These sessions usually include such topics as affirmative action, Right-to-Know legislation, sexual harassment, child abuse, and HIV. Develop a schedule for the year, and ensure that all faculty members are aware of the dates and topics.

Additional Notes: _____

_____

✳ *Staff Development*

Most districts provide a number of training days for staff during the year. The principal should see these as an opportunity to address buildingwide needs and concerns. A staff survey to identify topics for these programs is helpful. Designing the day so that staff members who do not regularly have the chance to interact do so will help break down the traditional departmental barriers that develop in high schools.

Additional Notes: _____

_____

✳ *National Honor Society*

The selection of students to the National Honor Society should follow the national guidelines and be directed by a local set of bylaws. Attention to this yearly task will help prevent controversies and problems. The principal should meet with the advisor and faculty council to review the selection process to ensure fairness and to anticipate any potential problems. (See Resource H—National Honor Society Selection Process.)

Additional Notes: _____

_____

* Sports Teams

Just as a principal needs to develop a schedule of class visits and observations, he or she should also develop a schedule to attend a balance of athletic events. Be sensitive to those sports traditionally ignored, whether they feature male or female students. Attending these events is a great opportunity to interact with parents and members of the community.

Additional Notes: _____

_____

September Personnel

* Start-of-School Materials

One way to avoid an opening faculty meeting that reviews all of the little details is to mail faculty their handbooks and special memos a week before school begins. While not all faculty members will read these in advance, many of your staff will appreciate the opportunity to concentrate on getting their rooms and materials ready rather than sitting in a long and boring opening meeting.

Additional Notes: _____

_____

* Emergency Information

Have the school secretary make updating and distributing the staff emergency phone chain a priority at the start of school. The chain is a valuable tool to use in weather emergencies or when a personal or schoolwide crisis occurs.

Additional Notes: _____

_____

* Teacher Observations

Evaluation of the teaching staff is one of the most important responsibilities of the principal. Develop a plan to ensure that all district and state deadlines for teacher observations and evaluations are met. Meet with all supervisors to review the format and process for evaluating teachers. All too often, teacher incompetence hearings are lost because a mistake was made in the process. Careful planning will avoid this and focus attention on the real issue: improving the quality of teaching in the classroom.

Additional Notes: _____

_____

✱ *"Sunshine" Committee*

The principal is the symbolic leader of the school staff, which should itself be thought of as a large family. As in any family, key events should be acknowledged. The principal should work closely with the "Sunshine" Committee to deal with both the good and the bad that staff members encounter in their personal lives. Keep a supply of sympathy, thank-you, congratulation, and birthday cards on hand.

Additional Notes: _____

_____

✱ *Administrative Staff Objectives*

Each member of the principal's administrative team should be expected to develop objectives and/or goals for the year. The principal should provide a general direction for the creation of these objectives, and should meet with each team member individually to approve them for the year. An end-of-year meeting to assess progress toward the objectives should be a regular part of the evaluation process.

Additional Notes: _____

_____

✱ *School Directory*

Creating and distributing a school directory to parents and students is a service that your community will appreciate. The directory should include important school, district, and community telephone numbers, as well as a list of students by grades, with their addresses and telephone numbers. Remember to give families the opportunity to opt out of the directory for privacy reasons.

Additional Notes: _____

_____

✳ *Counselors*

The week before school begins is often the most busy and hectic of the year. Providing an additional week for the guidance staff to prepare and bringing them into the school during this week will help ensure a smooth start to the school year.

Additional Notes: _____

_____

September Checklists

September Key Tasks

Major Assignments	Date Started	Date Completed	Days on Task
Conduct the first faculty meeting			
Conduct "dry runs" for the opening of school			
Meet with security staff and faculty supervisors			
Oversee the orientation of new students			
Meet with new teachers			
Complete reports for the superintendent			
Provide orientation for all those who use the public address system			
Meet with all cocurricular advisors to review expectations and procedures			
Hold required safety drills			
Begin student spirit-building activities			
Complete annual grant proposals			
Collect department staff development plans			

September Communications

	Assignment
	Compose a weekly memo to the staff
	Make personal visits to classes to emphasize expectations for student behavior
	Report to the PTA, superintendent, and board of education on school opening
	Send Open School Night invitations to all parents
	Write an article for the parent newsletter
	Write and distribute a memo to faculty on special education accommodations
	Develop public relations materials and activities for the National Merit semifinalists and commended students
	Send deficiency letters home to students who are missing required immunizations
	Attend monthly CST and PPS meetings to discuss problem students

September Planning

	Assignment
	Develop assembly procedures and plans
	Prepare for Open School Night
	Develop a calendar of monthly meetings
	Establish a schedule for guidance newsletters
	Maintain and review the student activities meeting calendar
	Schedule a Meet-Your-Coaches Night
	Schedule required inservice faculty meetings
	Plan for buildingwide staff development activities
	Meet with the National Honor Society advisor to review the selection process
	Develop a schedule to attend at least one contest for each sports team

September Personnel

	Assignment
	Mail start-of-school materials to the faculty
	Distribute the staff emergency telephone chain
	Establish a schedule of teacher observations and evaluations in coordination with assistant principals and department chairpersons
	Meet with the faculty "Sunshine" Committee to plan activities for the year
	Review written objectives with each member of the administrative staff
	Secure residence data to develop the school directory
	Budget an additional week for counselors before school opens

SEPTEMBER CALENDAR

MONTH: SEPTEMBER

YEAR: _____

MONDAY	TUESDAY	WEDNESDAY	THURSDAY	FRIDAY	SATURDAY / SUNDAY

Notes: _____

Ricken, R., Simon, R., & Terc, M. The High School Principal's Calendar. © 2000. Corwin Press, Inc.

Chapter Four

Don't find fault. Find a remedy.
Henry Ford

George Melton, a former leader of the National Association of Secondary School Principals, once said that a high school principal might *view* himself or herself as being a VIP. He did not, however, agree that principals are Very Important Persons, but asserted rather that the principal should be a leader with Vision, Integrity, and Passion. Helping a principal to become this type of VIP is what this calendar is all about.

If school opens smoothly in September, our passion for excellence and dedication to detail is amply rewarded. There are those who exhale and believe that October will be a lull before the increased tempo of the November and December holiday excitement, but we strongly differ in our point of view. The pace you have set must be maintained and your planning accelerated to harness the energy needed to meet your high expectations for the entire first semester.

In October, your faculty and students will ideally have settled into the established school routines. One look at the key tasks should be enough to focus on the challenges ahead. Three tasks usually dominate our thoughts. First, there is usually an Open School Night for parents. Our desire here is to showcase our excellent staff, course offerings, and physical plant, while nurturing a positive relationship with students' parents. Second, we usually send home our first interim report on student progress. These, as we will see, inform family members about their children's academic progress and behavioral conduct. Finally, there is planning for Halloween. We believe that planning some constructive activities around Halloween, even at the high school level, can help prevent a destructive incident. The challenge is to harness the energy and excitement for a worthwhile activity.

October Key Tasks

✳ Interim Reports

Regular communication between teachers and parents about a student's academic progress is vitally important. Interim reports should provide comments and feedback that are both positive and negative, as appropriate. Having a parent sign and return the report prevents later stories that a copy was never received. Remember to review a sample of these reports to ensure their quality and appropriateness.

Additional Notes: _____

_____

✳ Open School Night

Careful planning for the Open School Night is critical to the success of the evening. Ensure that the school looks good, extra student schedules are available, and plenty of coffee and refreshments are provided in the cafeteria. Use one of your student service groups to provide guides to help parents find their way around the school.

Additional Notes: _____

_____

✳ Budget Development

Developing the budget is a long and detailed process. Therefore, remember to give your department chairpersons as much lead time as possible. Provide a clear timeline of meetings, review sessions, adjustments, and so forth. Set conceptual parameters, and ask that new programs and additional staffing needs be handled separately from the routine budget needs.

Additional Notes: _____

_____

✳ *Testing Program*

Work with the staff coordinating your standardized testing program to develop a comprehensive schedule for the year. Put yourself in the shoes of the students taking the tests to ensure that tests have been scheduled on the calendar at times that do not conflict with other major school events and activities. Plan for the sharing of results with students, parents, and staff.

Additional Notes: _____

_____

✳ *Halloween*

Work with your student government officers to plan a positive activity for Halloween weekend. Just to be safe, however, add overnight security to monitor the building; taking extra precautions will save a lot of headaches.

Additional Notes: _____

_____

✳ *Senior Year Planning and Review*

Meet with your senior-class advisor to plan and review the major events for the year. These should include fundraising activities, the senior class trip, class photographs, ring sales, the yearbook, and, of course, the prom. Plan to hold a meeting of the entire class to set the tone for the year and to establish clearly your behavioral expectations for the year's many special events.

Additional Notes: _____

_____

✳ *Homecoming*

A successful homecoming weekend provides a real boost to school spirit. Monitor all plans for your homecoming with safety, good sportsmanship, and clean fun in mind. Send a special letter home to share plans for the event and to remind all of safety and expectations; doing so is a good way to prevent problems from occurring. (See Resource I—Homecoming Parade Memo.)

Additional Notes: _____

_____

✳ *Board of Education Recognition*

The high school is often the most visible building in the district, but, all too often, it is left out of plans for the traditional board of education Recognition Day. Be sure to plan events that showcase your students' many talents, interests, and services to the community. Invite board members to visit classes, sit in on a panel about local government, or discuss activities that highlight the service board members provide to the district.

Additional Notes: _____

_____

✳ *Emergency Drills*

A principal must attend to the required fire and emergency drills. Be proactive, and invite the local fire and emergency officials to attend one of your drills to give you feedback and suggestions. Make the first drill the best drill, because it sets the tone for the rest of the year.

Additional Notes: _____

_____

October Communications

✳ *Guidance Program and Planning*

Meet regularly with your guidance director to coordinate the many guidance events for the year. Transition programs are extremely important, and, as the school leader, you should welcome students and parents to each of these events. A positive guidance program will give parents confidence in the school and an assurance that their children will be well served.

Additional Notes: _____

_____

✳ *Board of Education Presentation*

Identify programs that the board and community should learn about. Work with the appropriate staff to prepare and deliver a presentation on each program at a board of education meeting. Not only will the board be more supportive, but the local press will also typically provide positive coverage in the paper.

Additional Notes: _____

_____

✳ *PTA Meetings*

The principal should meet regularly with the PTA leadership to help plan their monthly meetings. Such things as suggesting staff to speak and coordinating fundraising efforts are all part of a successful PTA. As principal, you should report at each meeting on the major events and issues that parents are interested in and concerned about. This is a great time to put to rest those rumors that always develop.

Additional Notes: _____

_____

✳ *Principals' Meetings*

A monthly meeting with the principals of your feeder school is a great way to improve articulation and students' transition to the high school. Not only will you have a good sense of the students coming to you each year, but you can also work with the other principals to address whatever problems come your way. As an added note, we encourage you to applaud the work of the elementary and middle school teachers when your students receive academic awards. Letting your community know that all the schools helped to prepare the students will ensure a positive relationship with the other schools.

Additional Notes: _____

_____

✳ *Local Service Clubs*

As principal, you have a responsibility to be the chief public spokesperson for the school. Joining your area service clubs, sharing school news, and providing students to help with community activities often pays dividends in the form of donations of money and equipment, as well as in the form of support for the budget and school in general.

Additional Notes: _____

_____

✱ *Bulletin Boards*

Develop a schedule for the use of bulletin boards and showcases around the building. Student clubs and organizations should be given responsibility for many of the displays. A building that looks good to the eye makes a positive first impression on visitors and parents.

Additional Notes: _____

_____

✱ *Freshman Orientation*

Providing a yearlong freshman orientation program will make for a successful transition of students from the middle school to the high school. Topics to cover in the orientation should include activity and club opportunities, student government, school rules and regulations, and the athletic program. The participation of guidance counselors should provide for an overview of the academic opportunities that your school has to offer.

Additional Notes: _____

_____

✱ *Thank-You Notes*

A principal can never send enough thank-you notes. Establish a system with your secretary to do this, and personalize as many notes as possible.

Additional Notes: _____

_____

✱ *School Profile*

Updating the school profile and test data fact sheet keeps community members, colleges, and employers supplied with the most current information about your school. Staff members should have copies, because they often are called on to be informal public relations ambassadors at community gatherings, events, or while shopping at the local mall.

Additional Notes: _____

_____

October Planning

✳ Capital Budget

Develop a five-year list of capital improvement projects to address the building needs you deem important. This list should be updated annually with the district's director of capital projects.

Additional Notes: _____

_____

✳ Fall Pep Rally

The first pep rally of the year is the most important, because it will set the tone for all that follow. Work closely with the staff member in charge of the event to ensure that all safety concerns are addressed.

Additional Notes: _____

_____

✳ American Education Week

American Education Week is a time to invite members of the community into your school to see the best that you have to offer. Showcase your top academic students, and provide each visitor with a packet of material to educate them about your strengths and needs as a school.

Additional Notes: _____

_____

✳ Principals' Organizations

Joining the local principals' or administrators' organization is a must. Attend at least one meeting a year. Networking will give you a local support base and a friendly voice to use as a sounding board about problems you face.

Additional Notes: _____

_____

October Personnel

* *Teacher Observations*

Read every teacher observation written by your administrative staff. By doing so, you will not only have a good handle on your staff, but will also be able to make these documents a part of your evaluation of each department chairperson and director.

Additional Notes: _____

_____

* *Staff Breakfast*

A principal needs to attend to the social side of the staff. Holding periodic, informal staff breakfasts is a way to bring the faculty together.

Additional Notes: _____

_____

October Checklists

October Key Tasks

Major Assignments	Date Started	Date Completed	Days on Task
Review student interim reports			
Prepare for Open School Night			
Set budget development timelines and parameters			
Coordinate testing program for the year			
Plan a Halloween dance or alternative activities			
Hold a planning meeting with the senior-class advisor			
Plan for the Homecoming parade and activities			
Coordinate your board of education Recognition Day			
Conduct fire and emergency drills			

October Communications

	Assignment
	Coordinate events with the guidance director
	Plan for the monthly board of education presentation
	Help plan the monthly PTA meeting
	Schedule meetings with elementary and middle school principals
	Plan to attend meetings of local service clubs
	Review the bulletin boards and school exhibits
	Prepare orientation sessions for parents and students of freshman class
	Send thank-you notes to groups who helped with Open School Night
	Update your school/student test data fact sheet and the school profile

October Planning

	Assignment
	Prepare a list of capital improvements for the budget process
	Monitor planning for the fall pep rally
	Plan American Education Week activities
	Schedule dates for the area principals' meeting on your calendar

October Personnel

	Assignment
	Check on the teacher observation process
	Hold a breakfast for staff

OCTOBER CALENDAR

MONTH: OCTOBER

YEAR: _____

MONDAY	TUESDAY	WEDNESDAY	THURSDAY	FRIDAY	SATURDAY / SUNDAY
___	___	___	___	___	___ ___
___	___	___	___	___	___ ___
___	___	___	___	___	___ ___
___	___	___	___	___	___ ___
___	___	___	___	___	___ ___

Notes: _____

Ricken, R., Simon, R., & Terc, M. The High School Principal's Calender. © 2000. Corwin Press, Inc.

Chapter
Five

Problems are only opportunities in work clothes.
Henry J. Kaiser

*I*n November, calm and routine should have replaced the hectic pace of the opening months of school. First report cards are a priority at this time, as students and staff come face-to-face with the reality of the school year.

Although promoting the academic environment is clearly a priority, November, which culminates with the Thanksgiving Day vacation, is also an important time for schoolwide service projects. Many school districts across the nation are adopting community service requirements to qualify for high school diplomas. The politics of these requirements aside, no one can debate the value of inculcating this ideal.

November is also a time when classroom visitations should be in full swing. Although we never minimize the importance of this process for all staff members, we urge that nontenured teachers be given priority. Within a few months, principals will have to make rehiring and tenure recommendations. Some contracts afford staff members several months notice if they are to be dismissed. Reality dictates that, as early as November, the principal or chairperson may have only three or four months left to make this critical recommendation. Know your contract, and observe faculty members early and often.

November
Key Tasks

★ NOVEMBER

✳ Faculty Meeting

Faculty meetings can easily become routine and boring to teachers. Make the faculty meeting a combination of "feel good" announcements about staff and intellectually stimulating presentations. Provide short readings as preparation for discussions on current topics and controversies. Bring community speakers in. Ask for feedback, and involve the staff in planning the meeting.

Additional Notes: _____

_____

✳ Teacher Observations

Make time in your schedule each week to conduct at least one formal observation and to visit a variety of classes informally. Remember to follow up on each visit with a short note to the teacher. Let your faculty know up front your approach and philosophy concerning observations and visits. Remember that recognizing the time when you should not enter a classroom is as important as making visits themselves.

Additional Notes: _____

_____

✳ Review Grades

Review the first marking period grades by teacher and department. Pay special attention to situations where there is an unusually high number of failing grades; work with the department chairperson to address and understand the circumstances producing such grades.

Additional Notes: _____

_____

✳ School Play

The school play is a wonderful opportunity to showcase the talents of your students and staff. It can also, however, be a flash point for controversy and problems. Advance work with the play advisor, a review of the script, and a preview by attending a rehearsal will give you the opportunity to address any problems before they become public issues.

Additional Notes: _____

_____

✳ School Service Projects

More and more students recognize the importance and value of participating in service projects. Colleges view such involvement as important, and potential employers see such participation as indicative of a positive work ethic. Coordinate such service activities, and make it a point to use the impact of student service to benefit the school as well as the community.

Additional Notes: _____

_____

November Communications

✳ PTA Presentation

Use your monthly PTA presentation to share plans for upcoming events and to ask for parental help and input on important projects and issues. By involving parents on a regular basis, you will ensure support at budget time.

Additional Notes: _____

_____

✳ Holiday Issues

One of the most sensitive and potentially explosive issues that principals face is handling holiday parties, decorations, sales, and so forth. Make it a point to be familiar with the district policies that govern each of these issues. Monitor all displays, concert programs, and similar items to ensure that policies are followed. Sending out a yearly reminder memo to all staff that spells out the key expectations will help to avoid problems later.

Additional Notes: _____

_____

✳ Board of Education Presentation

Use the monthly board of education meeting to recognize students and staff for the awards they receive. The board will relish the opportunity to congratulate students and staff for their special accomplishments.

Additional Notes: _____

_____

✳ *Promote Cultural Diversity*

Use the holiday spirit to promote cultural diversity and the appreciation of other religions. Make this a part of the instructional program to avoid any issues about the separation of church and state. One school that we know sponsors an annual Intercultural Unity Festival, which features foods and dances of the cultures represented in the school and the community population.

Additional Notes: _____

_____

✳ *Student Service Awards*

Develop a student-of-the-month award program. Provide the local press with a picture and a brief article about each student. Such programs promote school spirit and put your school in a positive light with the community.

Additional Notes: _____

_____

November Planning

✳ *Enrollment Projections*

As part of the budget and capital project development process, it is important to develop an accurate enrollment projection. Work with the middle school to obtain up-to-date figures for the incoming class, and monitor transfer numbers to make the appropriate adjustments. An accurate enrollment projection will give you credibility with the superintendent and the board.

Additional Notes: _____

_____

✳ *Freshman Orientation Review*

Run additional freshman orientation sessions. November is the time to solicit feedback from first-year students and to make adjustments to the program for next year. One principal lunches with the students at least once a week to gain valuable informal feedback on transition issues.

Additional Notes: _____

_____

✳ *Community Events*

This is the time of year to schedule events that open the school up to the community. Reach out to senior citizens by inviting them to special lunches, concerts, and activities. Indeed, many schools provide seniors with passes to all school events. One high school designates the dress rehearsal for the school play as a free show for all the senior citizens in the community.

Additional Notes: _____

_____

✳ *Professional Development Conferences*

Now is the time to apply for permission and funds to attend professional conferences. Attending such meetings is an important way to network, to stay on top of key trends, and to recharge one's batteries. The American Association of School Administrators (AASA) and NASSP national conferences, usually held in February or March, offer a variety of workshops. A weeklong summer institute, such as the Harvard Principals' Institute, can supply ideas and materials for years to come.

Additional Notes: _____

_____

✳ *Inclement Weather Procedures*

Review procedures for inclement weather, late openings, school closings, and early dismissals. Be sure that the snow telephone chain is up-to-date and distributed well before the first snowflake falls.

Additional Notes: _____

_____

November Personnel

✳ *Media/Library Services*

The library and media center should be the heart of a high school. Work with the librarian to plan a series of events and programs that encourage the use of the resources available in the library. These events might include author book talks, special displays, a book fair, or publishing summer reading lists.

Additional Notes: _____

_____

November Checklists

November Key Tasks

Major Assignments	Date Started	Date Completed	Days on Task
Conduct the monthly faculty meeting			
Do teacher observations			
Review grades by teacher and department			
Preview the school play			
Encourage schoolwide service projects			

November Communications

	Assignment
	Prepare a PTA presentation
	Compose a policy memo regarding holiday party, decorations, sales, and so forth
	Prepare a board of education presentation
	Foster the appreciation of other religions and cultures
	Initiate a student service awards program

November Planning

	Assignment
	Complete enrollment projections
	Schedule a second freshman orientation session
	Schedule the holiday dance, an art show, and community service events
	Apply for funds and permission to attend conferences
	Review the procedures for inclement weather

November Personnel

	Assignment
	Promote the use of media/library services

Ricken, R., Simon, R., & Terc, M. The High School Principal's Calender. © 2000. Corwin Press, Inc.

NOVEMBER CALENDAR

MONTH: NOVEMBER

YEAR: _____

MONDAY	TUESDAY	WEDNESDAY	THURSDAY	FRIDAY	SATURDAY / SUNDAY

Notes: _____

Ricken, R., Simon, R., & Terc, M. The High School Principal's Calendar. © 2000. Corwin Press, Inc.

Chapter
Six

Deeds not words.
Mother Teresa

A few red flags should be raised at this time to remind the principal about legal requirements and plans for the post-holiday period. Check fire inspection requirements, because principals are often required to send letters of compliance at the end of December and in June.

Setting schedules for midterm examinations cannot wait for your return in January. We recommend that copies of all formal examinations be submitted in December for review by the appropriate chairperson or building administrator.

The vacation period, depending on custodial vacation schedules, is an excellent time to complete some building projects, to have rooms painted, and to carry out a thorough cleaning of the facility. A meeting with the head custodian is essential to ensure a maximum effort from the staff when the students are not in attendance.

December
Key Tasks

* *Review*
   Budget Proposals

> The cost of educating children in the United States increases every year. Work with the board of education by providing clear and specific justification for each budget request, which can happen only with the cooperation, understanding, and hard work of the department chairpersons. Review each request with a public eye; preparation and planning will give the overall budget a strong foundation.

Additional Notes: _____

_____

* *Holiday Work Schedule*

> Take advantage of the holiday school closing to complete those projects that never seem to be finished. Work closely with the head custodian to ensure that priorities are addressed and the building is ready for the New Year. (See Resource J—Use of Building Memo.)

Additional Notes: _____

_____

* *Year-End Reports and New Goals*

> Complete all reports due at the end of the calendar year. Use this review as an opportunity to set goals to improve on the past year's performance. Share the information with the appropriate staff, and give recognition for jobs well done.

Additional Notes: _____

_____

* *Faculty Meeting*

> The December faculty meeting is a great time to celebrate with your staff. Using part of the meeting for a cookie swap or some other holiday activity promotes staff spirit.

Additional Notes: _____

_____

✳ *Classroom Observations*

Before the end of December, all nontenured staff should have been observed by the principal at least once. Observation is especially important in those cases where there is a question about rehiring a staff member. Even though the department chairperson may write a teacher's evaluation, the principal is expected to make the hiring recommendation; having completed a firsthand observation of such a teacher gives the principal far more credibility when questions arise.

Additional Notes: _____

_____

✳ *Variety Show*

Most schools hold some type of student variety show in December. Remember to preview the acts to avoid inappropriate themes or mishandling of sensitive issues. If some form of judging is involved, be sure to have a process that makes the selection of winners a fair one.

Additional Notes: _____

_____

✳ *Middle School Orientation*

It is not too early to begin the orientation and transition of students from the middle school to the high school. An initial evening meeting for parents and students is a good way to initiate the process. Make this a fun and upbeat evening: One school in New Jersey concludes the program with a game show event that reviews the important information covered at the meeting. (See Resource K—How to Help Memo.)

Additional Notes: _____

_____

✳ *Winter Pep Rally*

December is a great time to kick off the winter athletic season with a pep rally. Involve students in planning the event, and remember to give every team equal time and exposure. Hold the rally at the end of the day so that students will take the spirit and energy onto the field of play rather than into the classroom.

Additional Notes: _____

_____

December
Communications

✳ *PTA Presentation*

This is the time of year to begin planning the annual PTA Faculty Recognition Lunch and traditional fundraising events. Monitoring all the club and organization fundraising plans will avoid duplication and conflicts over dates and events. The PTA should receive preference, because they represent all of the parents in the school.

Additional Notes: _____

_____

✳ *Board of Education Meeting*

Carefully review the board of education agenda each month to anticipate questions that may be asked and to secure the necessary backup information and materials that may be called for. Alert the superintendent to any issues that you think may be raised from the floor, and be prepared to respond in an appropriate and thoughtful way. Quick thinking and preparation on the part of the principal often prevents questions and concerns from becoming problems.

Additional Notes: _____

_____

✳ *Course Catalog*

Revise and update the course catalogue used by students and parents to make program selections. This booklet should be well written and well organized. Provide local realtors, college officials, and employers with copies to emphasize the academic strengths of the school.

Additional Notes: _____

_____

✳ *Financial Aid Workshop*

Compose and send out letters inviting the parents of seniors to attend a financial aid workshop. Completing the financial aid form is often a scary prospect for parents. Providing parents with a workshop that takes them through the process and form in a step-by-step manner will help all students obtain the maximum available aid for college.

Additional Notes: _____

_____

December Planning

✱ Midyear Exams

Complete the midyear exam schedule. All staff, parents, and students should receive copies of the schedule well in advance of the exam period. Use the monthly newsletter to provide parents with suggestions on how to help their child prepare for the exams.

Additional Notes: _____

_____

✱ Winter Concert Schedule

Monitor the December calendar carefully. It quickly fills up, and conflicts with other schools' programs and community-wide events should be avoided, if possible. Also, review the program for the music concert for appropriateness and length. As school music programs expand, some schools hold two winter concerts to avoid the long nights. Reminding parents of proper etiquette in your monthly letter will help make concerts a pleasant affair for all involved.

Additional Notes: _____

_____

✱ Honor Society Induction

Plan the date and program for the honor society induction. Monitor the selection process to ensure that all requirements are met. When questions arise, do not hesitate to consult with the national offices of the honor society; they can provide valuable advice and suggestions based on years of experience.

Additional Notes: _____

_____

✱ Locker Cleanup

This is the time of year to schedule days for hall locker cleanup. Coordinate with the custodians to provide extra trash cans in the halls. Ask teachers to check lockers to avoid problems later in the year.

Additional Notes: _____

_____

December Personnel

* *Gifts*

Principals often purchase gifts for secretaries and custodial staff during the holiday season. Remember to coordinate this with the other administrators so that feelings are not hurt and gift giving does not get out of hand. Some schools provide food and refreshments to the entire secretarial and custodial staff, rather than purchasing individual gifts. Other schools use this time as an opportunity to make contributions to charity in the name of the secretaries and custodians.

Additional Notes: _____

_____

* *Coaching Evaluations*

Review the fall coaching evaluations in preparation for the coming year's hiring decisions. Meet with the athletic director, and use the coaching evaluations as a basis to discuss the overall program. Attention in this area will help prevent problems from developing.

Additional Notes: _____

_____

December Checklists

December Key Tasks

Major Assignments	Date Started	Date Completed	Days on Task
Review budget proposals with department chairpersons			
Meet with the head custodian to plan holiday work schedule			
Complete all year-end reports			
Schedule the faculty meeting			
Schedule classroom observations			
Preview the variety show			
Begin middle school orientation program for students and parents			
Hold winter pep rally			

December Communications

	Assignment
	Prepare the PTA presentation
	Prepare a presentation for the board of education meeting
	Revise and update the course catalogue
	Compose a letter of invitation for a financial aid workshop

December Planning

	Assignment
	Establish the midyear exam schedule
	Review the winter concert schedule
	Schedule the honor society induction
	Schedule midyear hall locker cleanup days

December Personnel

	Assignment
	Coordinate the purchase of gifts for office and custodial staff
	Review fall coaching evaluations

Ricken, R., Simon, R., & Terc, M. The High School Principal's Calender. © 2000. Corwin Press, Inc.

DECEMBER CALENDAR

MONTH: DECEMBER

YEAR: _____

MONDAY	TUESDAY	WEDNESDAY	THURSDAY	FRIDAY	SATURDAY / SUNDAY

Notes: _____

Ricken, R., Simon, R., & Terc, M. The High School Principal's Calender. © 2000. Corwin Press, Inc.

Chapter Seven

*The pessimist sees difficulty in every opportunity. The optimist
sees opportunity in every difficulty.*
Winston Churchill

The vacation period is over, and the building principal should reestablish a businesslike set of expectations for the staff and the student body. A tone-setting welcome back presentation via the public address system and visits to many classrooms are techniques often employed by school leaders for this purpose. Reminding students that this is the end of the first semester and urging them to prepare for midterm examinations provides a clear and demanding, yet caring, message.

The principal should be organizing both the end-of-first-semester activities and finalizing second-semester schedules and staffing. Doing these tasks is an excellent example of how an administrator must operate in the present, yet always be cognizant of the forthcoming month, semester, plans, and activities. As we have stressed, completing the key tasks is critical to a principal's success. Caring and intent are admirable, but they will not achieve a functional environment without intense planning.

We recommend that principals institute a system to ensure that all first-semester staff evaluations are completed in a timely fashion. By now, the supervisory staff should be able to list teachers whose professional performance is in need of improvement. In the following two or three months, constructive plans should be offered to assist these teachers. If they are not to be retained, principals should know about these concerns in January and should be equally aware of the supervisory plans developed. In this manner, there should be no surprises, and teachers should be informed before the spring recess if they are not to be retained.

Many schools have parent conferences at this time. The first open house was to discuss the curriculum and review each teacher's expectations for the course and the students enrolled. This second conference is to review individual progress with the students' parents or guardians. We have no quarrel if the conference is held in January or February; however, parents have a right to be informed fully by midyear, particularly if their child is having academic or behavioral problems. We must do more than pay "lip service" to teacher-parent collaboration. More important, notifying parents eliminates the possibility that parents will feel they were not adequately informed that their child was in jeopardy of failing; planning, conferences, interim reports, and telephone calls must be employed to eliminate the above scenario.

January Key Tasks

✻ *Review Evaluations*

The midyear point is an important time to review staff performance and chairpersons' evaluations. Meeting individually with each nontenured teacher is an opportunity to build on that teacher's strengths and address any concerns. Frequent communication with the chairperson is critical in this area.

Additional Notes: _____

_____

✻ *Remedial Plans*

All teachers in need of improvement should be identified, and the principal should develop a remedial plan for improvement that conforms to appropriate union contract provisions. Providing release time for such teachers to observe peers, attend training programs, and so forth should be a part of such plans.

Additional Notes: _____

_____

✳ *Department Goal Review*

Meet with each chairperson to review his or her progress toward departmental goals for the year. Goals should be specific and driven by student achievement data. Limit the number of goals, because having too many often means that little of substance is accomplished. In addition, the goals should fit into an overall school context and philosophy, which the principal is responsible for establishing and monitoring.

Additional Notes: _____

_____

✳ *Curriculum Initiatives*

New course proposals and course revisions should be submitted to the superintendent and board of education for approval, because the scheduling cycle for the coming year is about to begin. Department chairpersons should be responsible for an ongoing process of curriculum evaluation and assessment in their disciplines. The principal must make sure that all appropriate regulations and policies are followed.

Additional Notes: _____

_____

✳ *Finalize Budget*

The budget for the coming year should be finalized by this point. Begin planning for the presentation to the board of education and community. Many principals now use computer-generated presentations to demonstrate the many uses of technology.

Additional Notes: _____

_____

✳ *Informal Class Visits*

Visibility among staff and students is necessary for an effective principal. Build time into your daily schedule to visit classes informally. Keep a checklist of teachers visited to ensure that each faculty member is seen.

Additional Notes: _____

_____

✳ *Faculty Meeting*

Most states require a variety of annual staff training sessions and reviews of important safety and health procedures. Use a portion of each faculty meeting to meet this requirement. Local and regional offices are often willing to provide speakers and/or materials to satisfy such training requirements. Typically, such training is in such areas as Right-to-Know legislation, sexual harassment, and bloodborne pathogens.

Additional Notes: _____

_____

✳ *Senior Prep*

Now is the time to make sure that all seniors are measured for caps and gowns. A special meeting with parents of seniors sets the tone and expectations for the spring and for end-of-year events. A written contract that specifies such things as expectations about behavior and dress helps to avoid arguments and problems at the close of the year.

Additional Notes: _____

_____

✳ *Examination Week*

Provide all staff with clear directions on handling examination procedures and issues. Remind students about the definition and consequences of cheating. Hold a meeting with all exam proctors to review expectations and policies.

Additional Notes: _____

_____

January Communications

✳ *Parent-Teacher Conferences*

Given the push to increase standards and graduation requirements, regular meetings between parents and teachers is even more important. Designing the school schedule to include at least one or two parent-teacher conference days fosters enhanced communication. The principal is responsible for creating a schedule that works for both parents and teachers, and that articulates the purpose and function of the conference itself.

Additional Notes: _____

_____

✳ *PTA Presentation*

This is the opportune time of year to present program changes and enhancements proposed for the coming year to the PTA. Parents can and should be the school's strongest supporters. Presenting this information will not only help parents to support the school, but will also help them to guide their children in the coming course selection process.

Additional Notes: _____

_____

✳ *Board of Education Meeting*

Use this month's board of education meeting to highlight the programs and departments that often receive little attention, such as art, business, and occupational education. Most parents and board members know little about the regional programs in careers and occupations that are available to students. Attention to the noncollege-bound student is an important part of all high schools.

Additional Notes: _____

_____

✳ *Elective Fair*

Holding an elective fair for students is an exciting way to begin the course selection process. Set clear guidelines for this event, however, so that departments do not compete with each other.

Additional Notes: _____

_____

✳ *Review Lunch Program*

Asking students for feedback on the quality of the lunch program and for suggestions is a great way to involve students and improve services for them.

Many schools have established deli bars, salad bars, and health meals as a way of engaging students in the life of the school.

Additional Notes: _____

_____

January Planning

* *Grants*

Many grants are available to supplement existing programs and initiate new programs. Remember to monitor all grant deadlines to ensure that all available resources are utilized. Network with area principals to learn about new opportunities.

Additional Notes: _____

_____

* *Assembly and Bulletin Board Schedules*

Well-planned and well-executed student assemblies are an important part of any school program. Attention to detail and careful scheduling will avoid disruptions and concern over the loss of instructional time. Avoid scheduling assemblies during the final two weeks of each marking period. Motivational bulletin boards give students an opportunity to express themselves and educate their peers; develop a schedule that gives all groups access to the bulletin boards and keeps the displays fresh.

Additional Notes: _____

_____

* *Alumni Day*

An alumni day program is a great way to share college, military, and employment experiences with students who are about to make the transition themselves. Designate a committee to plan the event, send letters to recent alumni inviting them to visit, and use the day as an opportunity to sign up alumni for the alumni association.

Additional Notes: _____

_____

✻ *Assess Freshman Orientation Program*

By midyear, the freshman orientation program should be winding down as the course selection process for the next year begins. Ask each freshman to complete a survey assessing the first semester of their high school experience, and use the suggestions from the survey to make improvements for next year. Save the funny comments to use as part of the commencement address for the class in four years.

Additional Notes: _____

_____

✻ *Course Selection*

The course selection process drives the creation of the master schedule and the staffing requests for the coming year. Accuracy and detail are, therefore, very important. Meet regularly with the director of guidance to monitor the process, and look for trends that signal a need for curriculum revision or change.

Additional Notes: _____

_____

January Personnel

✻ *Staff Needs*

Make final recommendations for the coming year's staffing needs. These recommendations should be based on student selection, curriculum needs, and individual and group test results. Begin to prepare for the staff recruitment and interview process.

Additional Notes: _____

_____

✻ *Complete Teacher Evaluations*

All required teacher evaluations should have been completed and sent to the superintendent by this time. Highlight those evaluations that indicate either a problem or exemplary performance.

Additional Notes: _____

_____

✳ *Complete Nonprofessional Staff Evaluations*

The principal must also oversee the evaluation of secretaries, custodians, monitors, and aides. Evaluations should be completed in a timely manner. The support staff is a critical part of any school's operation.

Additional Notes: _____

_____

January Checklists

January Key Tasks

Major Assignments	Date Started	Date Completed	Days on Task
Review staff performance and chairpersons' evaluations			
Create remedial plans for staff in need of improvement			
Review the progress toward each chairperson's goals			
Review each department's progress on curriculum initiatives			
Finalize budget requests			
Make informal class visits			
Conduct the faculty meeting			
Schedule cap and gown measurements for seniors			
Prepare the examination week schedule and a statement about expectations			

January Communications

	Assignment
	Discuss parent-teacher conferences
	Coordinate the PTA presentation
	Prepare for the board of education meeting
	Hold an elective course selection fair
	Get feedback from students on the school lunch program

January Planning

	Assignment
	Review ongoing grants to ensure that all deadlines are met
	Plan the spring assembly and bulletin board schedules
	Coordinate Alumni Day
	Assess the freshman orientation program
	Complete steps for course selection process

January Personnel

	Assignment
	Finalize recommendation for staff needs for next semester
	Send superintendent all first-semester teacher evaluations
	Complete nonprofessional staff evaluations

Ricken, R., Simon, R., & Terc, M. The High School Principal's Calender. © 2000. Corwin Press, Inc.

JANUARY CALENDAR

MONTH: JANUARY

YEAR: ____

MONDAY ___	TUESDAY ___	WEDNESDAY ___	THURSDAY ___	FRIDAY ___	SATURDAY / SUNDAY ___
MONDAY ___	TUESDAY ___	WEDNESDAY ___	THURSDAY ___	FRIDAY ___	SATURDAY / SUNDAY ___
MONDAY ___	TUESDAY ___	WEDNESDAY ___	THURSDAY ___	FRIDAY ___	SATURDAY / SUNDAY ___
MONDAY ___	TUESDAY ___	WEDNESDAY ___	THURSDAY ___	FRIDAY ___	SATURDAY / SUNDAY ___
MONDAY ___	TUESDAY ___	WEDNESDAY ___	THURSDAY ___	FRIDAY ___	SATURDAY / SUNDAY ___

Notes: _____

Ricken, R., Simon, R., & Terc, M. The High School Principal's Calender. © 2000. Corwin Press, Inc.

Chapter Eight

Character is a diamond that scratches every other stone.

Bartol

Secondary schools are unique. For many teachers, this month marks the start of a new set of classes; the second semester in technology, art, music, business, and health often is September revisited. As many schools adopt some form of block scheduling, teachers may face an entirely new set of students and courses in the second half of the year. The principal must motivate those who teach these classes. Doing so is a challenge.

The transition to the second semester will be smooth if the planning was effectively completed in December and January. Believe it or not, many principals now turn their planning toward developing the schedule for the following September. Our to-do list seemingly has a life of its own.

Some school districts, particularly those in cold climates, have begun to take off the week during the George Washington birthday celebration. This not only saves the cost of fuel, but also allows the custodial staff to clean the building and perform some maintenance projects. It is a plan worthy of consideration.

February
Key Tasks

* Nontenured Teacher Evaluations

Be sure to meet all deadlines and procedural requirements in completing nontenured teacher evaluations. Far too many decisions not to rehire are reversed because of procedural flaws. Give teachers in difficulty the opportunity to resign rather than go through the termination process.

Additional Notes: _____

_____

* Semester Transition

Once the new semester has started, review all class sizes, teaching assignments, and program changes. Some sections become either very small or too large as a result of schedule changes made during the first semester. Work with the guidance director to balance class sizes.

Additional Notes: _____

_____

* Plan Master Schedule

A well-conceived master schedule will provide both students and staff with the best possible program. Extensive preparation and planning is necessary to make this a reality. Begin working with key personnel to develop the master schedule. Schedule singleton courses and seniors first.

Additional Notes: _____

_____

* Faculty Meeting

Every faculty meeting should provide some open time for faculty questions, concerns, and announcements. Place a clear time limit on this part of the agenda, or it may dominate the entire meeting. Work behind the scenes to encourage faculty to bring issues forward, even if you do not agree with them. Dialogue helps to air frustrations and sometimes generates creative solutions to problems.

Additional Notes: _____

_____

✳ Report Cards

By now, the second-quarter report cards should have been issued. Most report card formats provide room for a message from the school; make use of this space to remind parents of important upcoming events. The report card should also contain a grading key and/or explanation at the bottom, as well as a telephone number to contact if parents sense a mistake.

Additional Notes: _____

_____

✳ Grade Review

Use your review of grades by teacher and department to identify areas of concern. Contact teachers with unusually high failure rates and offer assistance, if appropriate. Keep the records on file and compare them on a year-to-year basis.

Additional Notes: _____

_____

February Communications

✳ Midyear Conferences

Meet with the department chairpersons to inspect class sizes for the new semester, survey plans for writing and producing final examinations, review the completion all teacher evaluations, and check on the status of the current year's budget and expenditures. This is also the time to discuss summer curriculum-writing projects.

Additional Notes: _____

_____

✳ PTA Presentation

Work with the PTA leadership to prepare for PTA officer elections and end-of-year events. It is a good practice to review the PTA bylaws on an annual basis to avoid any possible controversies.

Additional Notes: _____

_____

✳ *Board of Education Meeting*

Use the board of education meeting to share the special science and math research projects many of your students have entered in local, state, and national competitions. Involve the students in the presentations, and encourage them to engage the board members and audience directly.

Additional Notes: _____

_____

✳ *Government Letters*

Write the local elected officials and the president of the United States for letters of congratulations to graduating seniors. These letters make a great handout at the end-of-year awards ceremony and at graduation itself.

Additional Notes: _____

_____

✳ *Honor Roll*

Make it an annual practice to send students earning honor-roll status a letter of congratulation each marking period. Parents enjoy saving these letters, and students often make them a part of their college or job applications.

Additional Notes: _____

_____

✳ *Scheduling Student Conferences*

Once students have submitted their course requests for the coming year, individual meetings should be held between them and their guidance counselors to finalize these choices. The principal can learn of trends and issues by reviewing these meetings with each counselor.

Additional Notes: _____

_____

✳ *Students in Danger of Not Graduating*

When in doubt about whether a senior will graduate or not, send a registered letter to that student's parent. No principal wants to deal with upset parents who say in May or June that they had no idea their child might not graduate. Meet with the guidance staff to review all seniors to identify those who should receive such letters.

Additional Notes: _____

_____

February Planning

✶ *School Supplies*

Monitoring the status of school supplies on a regular basis prevents shortages from developing. Efficient record keeping will make the yearly budget process for supplies easier to justify and support. Many schools have begun to make purchases in bulk by joining educational cooperatives.

Additional Notes: _____

_____

✶ *Graduation Preparation*

The most visible and complicated event of the year is graduation. Literally thousands of people attend, and hundreds of details must be attended to. February is the time to update the list of things to do before graduation and to begin preparations for the big event. (See Resource L—Cap and Gown Letter.)

Additional Notes: _____

_____

✶ *Scheduling Input*

Department chairpersons play a central role in determining teacher and student schedules. Their input must come early and often during the scheduling process for it to be of use. Cooperation and advance planning will minimize student conflicts and place teachers in optimum assignments.

Additional Notes: _____

_____

✶ *Facilities and Grounds*

With the arrival of spring just around the corner, it is time to meet with the director of building and grounds to plan for the opening of spring sports and outdoor activities. An ongoing system of field maintenance and improvement will ensure that all teams have a safe and appropriate place to practice and play.

Additional Notes: _____

_____

February Personnel

**✳ *Assess New Teacher
    Orientation Program***

This is a good time of year to look back and assess the orientation program for new faculty. A survey of new teacher experiences will help design improvements to the process.

Additional Notes: _____

_____

✳ *Support Staff Meetings*

Regular meetings with the support staff will keep the office running smoothly. Look for opportunities to give secretaries and custodians public compliments and a few hours of time off before the end-of-year rush begins.

Additional Notes: _____

_____

February Checklists

February Key Tasks

Major Assignments	Date Started	Date Completed	Days on Task
Complete evaluations of nontenured staff members			
Evaluate the second-semester schedule and program changeover process			
Meet with key personnel about next year's master schedule			
Plan the monthly faculty meeting			
Issue second-quarter report cards			
Review teacher and departmental grades			

February Communications

	Assignment
	Hold midyear conferences with department chairpersons
	Prepare a PTA presentation
	Prepare the board of education report
	Write to government officials requesting letters of congratulation for graduates
	Send letters to high honor roll students
	Monitor individual student scheduling conferences
	Mail registered letters to seniors in danger of not graduating

February Planning

	Assignment
	Check on the status of school supplies
	Develop timelines for graduation preparation
	Establish due dates for chairpersons' scheduling input
	Coordinate preparation of facilities and school grounds for spring sports

February Personnel

	Assignment
	Evaluate the orientation program for new teachers
	Develop a dialog with support staff

FEBRUARY CALENDAR

MONTH: FEBRUARY

YEAR: _____

MONDAY	TUESDAY	WEDNESDAY	THURSDAY	FRIDAY	SATURDAY / SUNDAY
___	___	___	___	___	___ ___
___	___	___	___	___	___ ___
___	___	___	___	___	___ ___
___	___	___	___	___	___ ___
___	___	___	___	___	___ ___

Notes: _____

Ricken, R., Simon, R., & Terc, M. The High School Principal's Calender. © 2000. Corwin Press, Inc.

Chapter Nine

I touch the future. I teach.
Christa McAuliffe

Depending on the efficiency of the school district and the tenure of teachers' contracts, many high priority activities should be in operation. The start of the new teacher hiring process, the completion of the high school's budget proposals, the beginning of the upcoming year's master schedule, and the final phase of the incoming freshman orientation program are but a few.

Much attention should be paid to the third marking period. Interim reports should be sent home early in the month. Although report cards will be finalized at the beginning of April, teachers must be made aware of the importance of these interim grades for all students, particularly seniors. By now, every possible failure should have been reported to the guidance staff and the high school principal for action in April. The intent here is to eliminate surprises in the event that a student does not fully meet graduation course, credit, or sequence requirements.

March
Key Tasks

MARCH

* Build the Master Schedule

Student course selections have by now been tallied and the number of class sections determined as part of the budget process; it is now time to begin building the master schedule. Creating the conflict matrix is the first step in determining the best arrangement to meet the requests of as many students as possible. Modern computer scheduling packages give the principal the ability to try many variations on a schedule. Taking the time at this stage to get this task done correctly prevents many problems from developing later in the process.

Additional Notes: _____

_____

* Defending the Budget

The principal must be an advocate for the resources to provide students and staff with the best possible program. Use the many sources of data available to defend the budget request with facts, facts, and more facts. Avoid comparing your budget to another school's, and focus on the needs of your students.

Additional Notes: _____

_____

* Teacher Evaluations

Using the evaluation process correctly is as important as the substance of the evaluations themselves. Ensure that each staff member has received a copy in writing of everything required, and have a second administrator sit in on any meetings at which the teacher has a union representative present. Follow each conference with a quick memo of record to the teacher with a copy to the teacher's personnel file.

Additional Notes: _____

_____

* Last Stage of Freshman Orientation

Use the final part of the freshman orientation program to prepare students for the many examinations and standardized tests that often fill the end of the year. Give parents handouts that include suggestions to help them prepare their children to face these challenges. A good night's rest, a healthy breakfast, and a positive attitude will help every student do his or her best.

Additional Notes: _____

_____

✳ *Fire and Safety Drills*

Complete as many of the required fire and safety drills as possible in April to minimize class interruptions during the final two months of the year. (See Resource M—Emergency Drills Memo.)

Additional Notes: _____

_____

✳ *Faculty Meeting*

Remember to publish an agenda for each faculty meeting at least one week in advance. Do not hold a meeting just to say that you had a meeting; it is better to cancel a meeting than to fill the time with material that could be shared through a simple memo. Busy faculty will appreciate your recognition of the time demands that they face.

Additional Notes: _____

_____

✳ *Special Events*

Experience shows that events like a Battle of the Bands are a source of conflict and behavior problems. Creating performance contracts and providing extra supervision can help to minimize problems.

Additional Notes: _____

_____

✳ *Accreditation*

Most high schools participate in voluntary accreditation programs, which require progress reports, demographic information, and updates on a periodic basis. Keep the school's accreditation current, and begin the planning process for reaccreditation well in advance.

Additional Notes: _____

_____

March
Communications

✳ *Student Placement*
   Recommendations

Each department provides individual student placement recommendations for the coming year. This can often be a source of friction between parents and the school if parents want access to advanced and honors courses for their children. A process that uses multiple indicators for admission to advanced programs helps to reduce this conflict.

Additional Notes: _____

_____

✳ *Summer Curriculum Proposals*

Districts provide funding and time for staff to revise and create new curricula over the summer. The principal should coordinate proposals for such projects, prioritize them, and submit them to the superintendent for approval.

Additional Notes: _____

_____

✳ *Supervising Closing Activities*

The end of the year is one of the busiest times for student activities and programs. Many faculty members will be needed to supervise these events. Give all faculty members the opportunity to volunteer for these positions, and create a schedule to ensure that every event is adequately supervised.

Additional Notes: _____

_____

✳ *Board of Education Meeting*

A presentation featuring the results of standardized testing is an annual expectation of the principal. Clear and comprehensive tables and graphs will help parents and board members understand the school's strengths and the areas in need of improvement. A handout with summary material is an important way to share the results.

Additional Notes: _____

_____

* *PTA Meeting*

Each year, the PTA raises funds to support the school program. Keep a list of materials, equipment, and special items that the school needs, and offer it when the PTA leadership asks what the school would like. Remember to thank the PTA publicly for its contributions and ongoing efforts in support of the school.

Additional Notes: _____

_____

March Planning

* *Advanced Placement Exams*

Each May, students take a variety of advanced placement exams. Planning the school calendar with this in mind will avoid conflicts later in the year. Since seniors take most of the exams, planning special activities to follow the conclusion of the exam period is a good practice.

Additional Notes: _____

_____

* *Summer School Preparations*

More and more students are being required to attend summer programs as standards are increased. The summer school course bulletin should be completed and prepared at this time, so that appropriate staffing and materials can be secured.

Additional Notes: _____

_____

* *Closing Preparations*

Closing school is a complicated and detail-laden process. Checklists for each administrator and a comprehensive teacher checkout sheet should be prepared at this time.

Additional Notes: _____

_____

* *Scholarship Awards*

A committee of teachers and administrators should coordinate the assignment of student awards and scholarships. This group should begin meeting in April to organize the annual awards assembly and to generate a list of graduate scholarship winners.

Additional Notes: _____

_____

March Personnel

* *Staff Recognition Lunch*

The PTA traditionally holds a staff recognition lunch. Make it a point to allow everyone to attend, and write the appropriate thank-you notes on behalf of the faculty.

Additional Notes: _____

_____

* *Cards and Notes*

Keep a supply of sympathy, get well, congratulation, and thank-you cards on hand to send to staff on important occasions. Have your secretary keep you up-to-date on social developments with the staff.

Additional Notes: _____

_____

* *Hiring New Staff*

Begin the new teacher hiring process by advertising at colleges and in newspapers. Screen applications by committee, and remember that a writing sample is a valuable article for the committee to consider. Involve the staff in the interview process, and invite semifinalists to teach a model lesson. Also, remember to check references carefully; often, what is *not* said in a reference is the most important piece of information. Recommend finalists to the superintendent.

Additional Notes: _____

_____

March Checklists

March Key Tasks

Major Assignment	Date Started	Date Completed	Days on Task
Begin work on the master schedule			
Prepare to defend your budget recommendations			
Complete all nontenure teacher evaluations and recommendations			
Finalize the last phase of the freshman orientation process			
Complete yearly fire and emergency drills			
Plan the monthly faculty meeting			
Oversee special school events			
Complete all accreditation activities			

March Communications

	Assignment
	Circulate department recommendations for student placement
	Collect summer curriculum development requests
	Request the name of teachers to supervise closing activities
	Plan the monthly board of education presentation
	Prepare a PTA meeting presentation

March Planning

	Assignment
	Establish the advanced placement examination schedule
	Complete the summer school bulletin with course options
	Revise the building-closing checklist and teacher checkout form
	Establish the scholarship and awards committee

March Personnel

	Assignment
	Host the staff recognition day lunch
	Send cards or notes to staff for key events
	Begin the hiring process for new teachers

Ricken, R., Simon, R., & Terc, M. The High School Principal's Calender. © 2000. Corwin Press, Inc.

MARCH CALENDAR

MONTH: MARCH

YEAR: _____

MONDAY	TUESDAY	WEDNESDAY	THURSDAY	FRIDAY	SATURDAY / SUNDAY

Notes: _____

Ricken, R., Simon, R., & Terc, M. The High School Principal's Calender. © 2000. Corwin Press, Inc.

Chapter
Ten

The object of education is to prepare the young to educate themselves throughout their lives.
Robert Maynard Hutchins

*T*he third-quarter marks should be sent this month, as should both congratulatory letters and warning letters to seniors whose graduation is in jeopardy. The work of the guidance department is most critical at this time; next year's programming demands should not detract from the counseling process. Students with multiple failures on their report cards should be required to meet with their guidance counselors. Remind students that working harder during the remaining ten weeks is better than studying the night before the final examination!

Ideally, the master schedule is in its final form. Staffing of classes, athletic teams, and clubs should all be winding down. We urge principals to give some thought to the effectiveness of the advisors and not to allow seniority to blind your professional judgment. Often, long-term activity advisors bring experience to the task, but lose their zest and creativity. An honest assessment is in order.

The high school budget is now being reviewed by the superintendent and the board of education. A personal presentation by a knowledgeable principal is the best way to minimize cuts to your proposals. Armed with specific reasons for each budget item, you should be a convincing and effective presenter.

April Key Tasks

APRIL

✳ *Master Schedule*

By this point in the year, the master schedule for the next year should be nearing completion. Remember to check each teacher's schedule to see that all contract requirements have been met. Review class sizes, and begin the balancing process.

Additional Notes: _____

_____

✳ *Graduation Preparation*

All materials and equipment for graduation should have been ordered by now. Meet with the senior-class officers to obtain their input on the program for the ceremony. Begin to identify student speakers and those who wish to perform a musical presentation at graduation. One school that we know of permits any senior to submit an essay to be read at graduation; a panel of faculty selects the best essays to be part of the ceremony.

Additional Notes: _____

_____

✳ *New Student Orientation*

This is a good month to hold an evening meeting for the parents of incoming ninth graders. The presentation should include an overview of each department's curriculum and a review of club and organization opportunities.

Additional Notes: _____

_____

✳ *Budget Presentation*

The public budget presentation for the coming year should focus on how the instructional needs of all students will be met. Highlight new programs and expenses, as well as savings and adjustments. Provide members of the audience with a one-page summary handout.

Additional Notes: _____

_____

✳ *Student Government Elections*

Monitor the student government election process. Each candidate should receive a written set of guidelines and instructions for the election process, as well as a statement of the responsibilities for the position. The student council advisor should preview all speeches.

Additional Notes: _____

_____

April Communications

✳ *PTA Presentation*

The April PTA meeting is a good time to review the major end-of-year activities and expectations. Give parents guidelines and suggestions for managing the prom weekend. Many local limousine companies will sign pledges to prohibit students from having alcohol or drugs in their vehicles. Providing parents with a list of these companies is an excellent public relations and safety step.

Additional Notes: _____

_____

✳ *Board of Education Meeting*

This is an appropriate meeting at which to share recent SAT/ACT results. Provide the board with a five-year summary of results and the appropriate comparisons to other like schools. Identifying how the curriculum supports students in preparing for these examinations will demonstrate the school's commitment to helping students get into the best possible colleges.

Additional Notes: _____

_____

✳ *Congratulations Letters*

Send out congratulation letters to students who earned honor-roll status during the last report card period. Some schools also provide a special breakfast for these students as recognition for their achievement.

Additional Notes: _____

_____

✳ *Spring Musical*

The preparation and staging of a schoolwide musical or play takes months of work on the part of staff and students. Make it a point to attend as many performances as possible and to send the director, staff, and performers a letter of commendation.

Additional Notes: _____

_____

✳ *Faculty Evaluations*

All teacher observations required as part of the yearly evaluation process should be completed by the first part of April. Use the remainder of the month to write and review all teacher evaluations. Use the evaluation conference as an opportunity to seek feedback on your own work as principal.

Additional Notes: _____

_____

✳ *Academic Warning Letters*

Do an updated review of the academic status of each senior, and send registered letters to each senior in danger of not graduating. In situations where it appears that there is no chance for the student to salvage the year, a parent conference to begin planning for other options, such as summer school or a GED diploma, should take place.

Additional Notes: _____

_____

✳ *Middle School PTA Presentation*

Keep the parents of the middle school apprised of the high school program through an annual presentation at a middle school PTA meeting. This will give you an opportunity to get to know the active parents who will soon be the leaders of your own school's PTA.

Additional Notes: _____

_____

April Planning

✻ *Vacation Schedules*

Develop a comprehensive calendar of summer work and vacations among the administrative team and building secretaries. Be sure that someone will be available in the building all summer to answer questions and to register new students. Remember to identify a few days when all administrators will be available to hold summer planning meetings.

Additional Notes: _____

_____

✻ *Senior Awards*

Meet with the senior-class awards committee to make sure that as many seniors as possible will receive recognition. Awards programs that recognize only a few students often result in upset parents.

Additional Notes: _____

_____

✻ *Transition Program*

Developing a transition program for seniors going off to college, the military, or work can provide a positive spring activity. Devoting a day to special presentations on topics appropriate to adjusting to adult life can be very meaningful.

Additional Notes: _____

_____

✳ *Cultural Arts Program*

The spring is an excellent time to promote the arts program by sponsoring a community-wide cultural arts festival. Art students can display their best work, while drama and speech students can offer performances. Music presentations should include the regular student groups along with an opportunity for individual recitals.

Additional Notes: _____

_____

✳ *Academic Awards*

An academic awards program should be held each year. The principal should review the program to ensure that as many students as possible receive some recognition. Service, attendance, and the arts should receive equal billing with academic accomplishments.

Additional Notes: _____

_____

April Personnel

✳ *Teacher Openings*

Developing a substantial pool of quality applicants for teacher openings is an increasingly difficult task. Establishing and maintaining contacts with area teacher colleges and, if needed, sending staff to recruiting fairs is necessary to secure the best possible candidates. Use both local and regional newspapers to place ads for the openings.

Additional Notes: _____

_____

✳ *Secretaries' Day*

The principal's job includes supervising a hard-working secretarial staff. Show just how important secretaries are by making the celebration for Secretaries' Day something special.

Additional Notes: _____

_____

April Checklists

April Key Tasks

Major Assignments	Date Started	Date Completed	Days on Task
Complete a draft of the master schedule for the coming year			
Continue graduation preparation activities			
Begin the orientation program for next year's freshmen			
Make a public presentation on the proposed budget for the high school			
Conduct the election for student government officers			

April Communications

	Assignment
	Update the PTA on end-of-year activities
	Attend the monthly board of education meeting
	Send letter of congratulation to third-quarter students with honor-roll status
	Congratulate the cast and crew of the spring musical
	Send a reminder to department chairs to complete faculty evaluations
	Contact the parents of seniors in danger of not graduating
	Give a presentation to the middle school PTA

April Planning

	Assignment
	Establish summer vacation/work schedules for the administrative team
	Schedule a meeting with the senior-class awards selection committee
	Establish a transition program for graduating seniors
	Facilitate the planning program for a cultural arts festival
	Develop a program for the annual academic awards assembly

April Personnel

	Assignment
	Place advertisements for anticipated staff openings
	Celebrate Secretaries' Day

Ricken, R., Simon, R., & Terc, M. The High School Principal's Calender. © 2000. Corwin Press, Inc.

APRIL CALENDAR

MONTH: APRIL

YEAR: _____

MONDAY	TUESDAY	WEDNESDAY	THURSDAY	FRIDAY	SATURDAY / SUNDAY

Notes: _____

Ricken, R., Simon, R., & Terc, M. The High School Principal's Calender. © 2000. Corwin Press, Inc.

Chapter Eleven

Tell me, I forget. Show me, I remember. Involve me, I understand.
Ancient Chinese proverb

The completion of all observations of staff by the end of this month is necessary if final evaluations are to be given before the summer vacation. We have always believed that, as part of the teacher's final evaluation, a discussion about specific goals for the upcoming year should take place. Some districts actually formalize this process. The value of such a discussion is that the staff member is made aware of the goals in the event that they wish to plan over the summer. It also allows for some inservice or college courses to be taken in July or August.

A complete review of the present year's budget is in order in May. Department chairpersons, teachers, and secretaries should be able to discuss each area's excess or shortfall. Ideally, this review was done several months earlier, while preparing the next school year's budget; however, we find an analysis at this time to be far more accurate for future planning.

If your district involves the teaching staff in the hiring of their future colleagues, this process should be in full swing by now. Whenever possible, we recommend that all candidates teach a model lesson when they become semifinalists for a position. Staff members who participate in hiring new teachers not only learn from the interviews, but also become proactive in helping the candidate when he or she joins the staff. Often, the teacher who interviews candidates becomes a willing mentor.

The checklist of tasks becomes a massive clerical job at the end of the school year. The signing of diplomas, award certificates, and student yearbooks are both legally necessary and emotionally satisfying to your graduates. However, finalizing evaluations, making hiring recommendations, fine tuning the master schedule, and ensuring the integrity of final examinations are essential to both the success of the present year and the start of the next. An error in May can create chaos in September. This constant dual responsibility is what makes high school principals special.

May Key Tasks

* Faculty Meeting

Faculty members are often tired and frustrated from a long school year. Plan to make the May faculty meeting an upbeat, fun experience. Engage faculty in an exercise that breaks from the bureaucratic routine. Poetry readings or a presentation on how to manage stress are topics that will be welcome at this point in the year.

Additional Notes: _____

_____

* Evaluation of Administrators

The evaluation of your administrative team should hold no surprises for anyone. Concerns should be addressed as they occur, and significant issues should be handled with frequent meetings and plans for improvement. Some principals have their assistant principals and department chairpersons complete a self-evaluation as part of this process.

Additional Notes: _____

_____

* Report on Goals

Each year, the high school has one or more goals to meet and has committees working on projects or standing issues. The principal should prepare a yearly report for the superintendent and board that identifies each goal and committee, and summarizes the accomplishments of the year. This report often is incorporated into the evaluation of the principal by his or her supervisor.

Additional Notes: _____

_____

* *Fire Drills*

All required fire and safety drills should have been completed by now, and the appropriate forms and reports submitted to the necessary parties. Use a year without any problems as an opportunity to recognize the fine work of the custodial and maintenance staff in this area.

Additional Notes: _____

_____

* *Exit Interviews*

Often, the best source of information on the quality of the program and staff comes from the students themselves. Schedule time during this month to meet with individual students or small groups of seniors to access their experiences. A follow-up written survey during the next year gives even more feedback about how well the students were prepared for college, work, or the military. These results can make for a very lively faculty meeting discussion. Remember to clear this activity with your union building representatives to avoid the appearance of "checking up" on the staff.

Additional Notes: _____

_____

* *Diplomas*

During May, it seems that the stack of certificates, diplomas, and other papers to sign just keeps getting larger. Use the time devoted to this task as an opportunity to think about each student as you sign his or her diploma or award certificates. How many do you know well? Finding that you do not know many students should serve as a motivation to spend more time directly with students.

Additional Notes: _____

_____

✳ *Standardized Tests*

As the standards movement strikes more and more schools, May is often the time when standardized tests are required. Work with the faculty to devise the optimum testing environment and adjust the school schedule of activities to give students as much rest as possible in the days leading up to the testing.

Additional Notes: _____

_____

✳ *Advanced Placement Exams*

Advanced Placement examinations are given annually during a two-week period in May. The scheduling of these tests is often a logistical challenge, because regular classes are going on at the same time. By moving some classes around, an isolated and secure testing room or rooms can be established.

Additional Notes: _____

_____

✳ *District Budget and School Board Elections*

Typically, school districts schedule their school board elections and voting on the annual budget in May. The high school is often the major polling site for the vote. Remember to follow all election rules, and provide the election volunteers with refreshments and administrative support. Smooth election procedures will help minimize controversy and problems.

Additional Notes: _____

_____

✳ *Senior Prom*

The prom is the social highlight of the year for students; it can also cause a principal the most headaches of the year. Work closely with the students planning the prom to ensure an appropriate location is selected. Many school SADD chapters offer a "no alcohol and drugs" contract designed for such activities as the prom. Ensure that adequate security and supervision are provided, and determine the procedures to follow if any problems develop.

Additional Notes: _____

_____

May
Communications

✽ *Closing Procedures*

The last day of the school year can be hectic and confusing if clear closing procedures have not been established and communicated. Work with the secretarial staff to design a sign-out process that prevents long lines and frustration. Make sure that all staff members provide you with a summer address. Many schools build a special fun faculty meeting into the last day as a closing activity. The end of the year is also a great time to recognize staff who have made special contributions. Ending the year on a positive note will help everyone return in the fall ready to start the year with enthusiasm.

Additional Notes: _____

_____

✽ *PTA Meeting*

Remember to use one of the final PTA meetings of the year to recognize publicly the officers of the PTA for their volunteer work and contributions to the school. Some principals keep a supply of school pins or T-shirts on hand to give as token gifts at such occasions.

Additional Notes: _____

_____

✽ *Board of Education Meeting*

Many schools have elected student representatives to the board of education. The principal should meet with these students regularly to review their concerns and issues. A few key words by these students at the right time can often influence the direction of the board.

Additional Notes: _____

_____

✽ *Progress Reports*

The final-quarter progress report is often the most important of the year. Many students, especially seniors, have difficulty maintaining their level of work as summer looms around the corner. Parents need to know if such a trend is developing so that they can intercede before it is too late.

Additional Notes: _____

_____

May Planning

❊ Activities Calendar

Developing the yearly calendar of activities is a complicated task. A special meeting devoted to this job should be held with all cocurricular advisors. The calendar should also be coordinated with the middle school and elementary school, because many parents have students at more than one school. Remember to note the days before each marking period is scheduled to end and any days set aside for special testing. A careful check of religious holidays will also avoid later problems.

Additional Notes: _____

_____

❊ Budget Analysis

May is an excellent month to review the year's expenditures. Note areas that have either overspent or did not expend their allotted funds, and make the appropriate adjustments for the following year. Being proactive in this area will serve you well throughout the budget process.

Additional Notes: _____

_____

❊ Spring Calendar

The principal's calendar is often a logistical nightmare. Work with the secretary to block out certain times for class visits and just wandering around the halls, and remember to put all major evening and weekend activities on the calendar. Although the principal does not have to attend every event, he or she should monitor the calendar carefully to avoid appearing to favor one type of activity over another.

Additional Notes: _____

_____

❋ Senior Portraits

The principal must be the chief guardian of instructional time. Schedule activities such as taking senior portraits for the summer so as not to take students out of classes. The faculty and parent community will respect and support this approach.

Additional Notes: _____

_____

❋ Schedule Class Elections

May is a good time to schedule class elections. A planning meeting with the class advisors and candidates will set the tone for a positive and well-run campaign and election. Send congratulation letters to the winners, and letters commending the losers for running. (See Resource N—Class Election Memos.)

Additional Notes: _____

_____

May Personnel

❋ Cocurricular Recommendations

Finding appropriate staff to fill the many co-curricular and coaching positions each year can be a challenge. Make it a point to give preference to your own teachers or those in the district. Also, remember that an interview and evaluation process for hiring cocurricular staff is just as important as it is when you hire a teacher. Completing your recommendations this month is important, because the final month of the year is far too busy to address this issue.

Additional Notes: _____

_____

❋ Hiring New Staff

Most of the teacher openings for the coming year should be filled by now. Waiting until the summer to complete this task makes filling the positions more difficult, because many staff members will not be available to participate in the process. A detailed recommendation, with at least two reference checks, will assist the superintendent in presenting the candidates to the board of education.

Additional Notes: _____

_____

✻ *Cocurricular Reports*

Require each cocurricular advisor to complete and submit an end-of-year report. This should include a list of meetings held, the number and names of students involved, and a summary of major activities accomplished. A financial accounting should also be included.

Additional Notes: _____

_____

✻ *Staff Recognition*

Recognizing staff is an important part of the symbolic role a principal plays. The recognition should be genuine, and should acknowledge all groups that work in the building. Pay particular attention at this time to retiring faculty and staff members, and recognize them for their length of service.

Additional Notes: _____

_____

May Checklists

May Key Tasks

Major Assignments	Date Started	Date Completed	Days on Task
Conduct the monthly faculty meeting			
Complete evaluations of the assistant principals and department chairpersons			
Prepare a report on goal completion and committee work			

Major Assignments	Date Started	Date Completed	Days on Task
Conduct any remaining fire drills			
Complete senior exit interviews			
Sign diplomas and award certificates			
Oversee the administration of standardized tests			
Monitor the administration of advanced placement examinations			
Oversee the district budget vote			
Attend the prom			

May Communications

	Assignment
	Complete and distribute the school-closing procedures
	Give a presentation at the PTA meeting recognizing parent volunteers
	Provide the board of education with an end-of-year report
	Issue fourth-quarter progress reports

May Planning

	Assignment
	Begin developing the activities calendar for the coming year
	Complete and analyze the present year's budget
	Plan to supervise and/or attend key spring events
	Coordinate scheduling and the taking of senior portraits
	Conduct class officer elections

May Personnel

	Assignment
	Submit recommendations for next year's cocurricular and coaching appointments
	Send hiring recommendations to the superintendent
	Complete a cocurricular activity report
	Recognize faculty and staff retirees for their length of service

MAY CALENDAR

MONTH: MAY

YEAR: _____

MONDAY	TUESDAY	WEDNESDAY	THURSDAY	FRIDAY	SATURDAY / SUNDAY

Notes: _____

Ricken, R., Simon, R., & Terc, M. The High School Principal's Calender. © 2000. Corwin Press, Inc.

Chapter Twelve

Children are the messengers we send to a generation we may never know.

Arlo Arth

Endings are hectic and emotional, and it is impossible to meet the time commitments required by the end-of-year activities without careful planning and help from the rest of the administrative staff. Culminating activities for clubs, service organizations, and athletic teams often take place outside the school day, and many organizations have dinners and banquets at local catering halls and restaurants. The principal should attend as many as possible or send an assistant principal or chairperson as his or her representative.

In school, the pace is even more frenetic. The monumental process of final examinations and closing activities is compounded by the need for an organized, orderly sign-out procedure. The key tasks for this time of year are almost unfair to list. A new administrator can easily be overwhelmed, because each requirement is absolutely necessary. Any letdown in the efficiency of performing these end-of-year activities will have a negative ripple effect in the summer and throughout the following school year. Think, for example, of the possible ramifications of the following oversights: retiring teachers failing to hand in classroom keys; incomplete health records for student athletes; misplaced final examinations; teachers not leaving summer addresses; purchase orders not signed; homeroom attendance records not submitted. We could continue. The teacher sign-out procedures, which must be completed before they can receive their final salary checks, must be planned and monitored by the high school administration. If something goes wrong, we all know where "the buck stops."

Our high school lists the following items that must be initialed by a chairperson or building administrator for each teacher before he or she can leave on summer vacation:

1. Class recordbooks

2. Attendance registers

3. Grade reports

4. Failure lists and final examinations

5. Permanent record cards

6. Textbook counts and locations

7. Report cards for absentees

8. Course outlines

9. Locker codes and locks

Items unique to a principal's school can be added as necessary.

The following key tasks validate our belief that high school principals are master planners. An annual miracle occurs when all tasks are accomplished in a timely fashion. We can delegate these tasks, but the final responsibility is our own. Good luck! We hope these ideas will serve as a "tickler file" to add to your own repertoire.

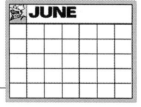

June Key Tasks

✳ Final Examinations

Each year, national surveys of top high school students reveal that cheating is widespread among all students. Make honesty a top priority during the administration of final examinations. Meet with the exam proctors to review expectations and procedures for handling possible cheating situations. Develop a statement to be read by each proctor before an examination begins. Be available to handle personally any serious situations that develop. Create a testing site that will discourage students from cheating.

Additional Notes: _____

_____

✽ *Final Report Cards*

Use the final mailing of report cards as an opportunity to give parents suggestions on how to help prepare their children for the coming school year. Make guidance counselors available for a few days immediately after report cards go home; they will be able to answer many of the questions and concerns parents may have. Inform parents of procedures involved in signing up their student for summer school courses.

Additional Notes: _____

_____

✽ *Review Final Grades*

The principal should prepare a comprehensive report for the superintendent reporting on the results of final examinations and grades. This report should also serve as an opportunity to meet with department chairpersons and specific teachers to improve instructional practices and adjust the curriculum. Keep all final examinations and teacher gradebooks on file. Parents and students may want to review the grading of a particular examination or grade.

Additional Notes: _____

_____

✽ *End-of-Year Reports*

Do not put off completing the many end-of-year reports required by your district and state. Double-check each report, because a small mistake may be compounded in any district or state reports that are made public.

Additional Notes: _____

_____

✽ *Locker Cleanout*

The final locker cleanout can also become part of the preparation process for the opening of the next school year. Have each homeroom teacher check each locker and report on any that need repairs or attention. Doing this will help the custodial staff concentrate its efforts on the areas that need the most attention. (See Resource O—Locker Cleanup Memos.)

Additional Notes: _____

_____

✳ *Graduation*

The principal sets the tone for graduation at the rehearsal and in communications made to the parents of seniors. Some schools that have experienced disruptions now require seniors to sign a contract for participation. Oversee the distribution of tickets and the production of the program. Triple-check the spelling and pronunciation of each senior's name to avoid embarrassing situations. Meet with all supervisory staff both before the ceremony to discuss responsibilities and afterward to generate suggestions for improving the next year's ceremony.

Additional Notes: _____

_____

✳ *Awards Assembly*

The annual academic awards program is often a long and drawn-out affair. Work with the presenters to keep the program moving. Remind all of behavior expectations, and provide everyone with a program list of the award winners after the event is over.

Additional Notes: _____

_____

✳ *Summer School Registration*

Provide all students and parents with the opportunity to register early for summer school. This will assist parents in planning for the summer and give the summer school administrator an idea of the number of students attending.

Additional Notes: _____

_____

✳ *Sign-Out*

The principal should publish a comprehensive end-of-year checklist for teachers. This should include a cover sheet with a list of materials that must be turned in for closeout and a place for the appropriate staff member to initial that an item has been submitted or a task completed. Set a distinct time for final checkout, and remember to work with the office staff to make this process go smoothly. (See Resource P—End-of-Year Checkout List.)

Additional Notes: _____

_____

❋ *Attend End-of-Year Events*

Keep your calendar clear during the last few days of school to handle the last-minute issues that almost always develop. Remember to schedule time to attend all of the closing events, and use these opportunities to speak to and to thank people for their contributions during the year.

Additional Notes: _____

_____

❋ *Summer Work*

Send your recommendations for summer curriculum writing, guidance hours, and summer staffing to the superintendent. Provide those teachers assigned to curriculum writing with models on which to base their work. Maximize your summer staffing to have as many days covered with at least one administrative staff member.

Additional Notes: _____

_____

❋ *Books and Equipment*

Collecting books and equipment is a major undertaking. Work with the staff to create a record-keeping system that is easy to use and understand. Notify parents of any outstanding books or equipment as soon as possible, and indicate the times and locations to return these items. Withhold diplomas of seniors who have not settled all their school-related accounts.

Additional Notes: _____

_____

June Communications

* Board of Education Presentation

The June board of education meeting is a time of transition. The newly elected board members are preparing to take office, and are anxious to learn about the schools. Use your presentation to highlight the major accomplishments of the year, and begin to identify the goals and special events coming in the next school year.

Additional Notes: _____

_____

* PTA Meeting

The annual PTA installation night is the principal's opportunity to acknowledge the most active and supportive parents. At the same time, parents want and respect a principal that tells it as it is. Balance the positive comments with an honest assessment of the areas that the school must continue to improve.

Additional Notes: _____

_____

* Summer Schedule

Communication is perhaps the most important function for which the principal is responsible. Continue to reach out to staff over the summer with letters and opportunities for direct contact. Let all staff members know your summer schedule, and invite them to visit at any time.

Additional Notes: _____

_____

* Staff Meetings

Use the calm pace of the summer to meet individually with staff members. Plan for these meetings by developing a list of questions that focus on both the broad concerns and issues that educators should be addressing and the problems and routine concerns they should be handling.

Additional Notes: _____

_____

June Planning

✳ *Final Exam Failures*

Make the reporting of final exam and final grade failures a priority. A personal call to parents with information about options will be appreciated. No parent should be surprised by a failure if teachers have done a good job with ongoing communication and the progress report system. Send home a written failure notice as well.

Additional Notes: _____

_____

✳ *Chaperones*

The many final activities of the year require the help and assistance of staff. Give everyone an opportunity to volunteer, and use your veteran teachers to serve as supervisors for the events.

Additional Notes: _____

_____

✳ *Summer Cleaning Schedule*

Meet with the head custodian to develop a summer cleaning schedule for the building. Remember to avoid conflicts with summer school and the start of fall sports. Check the condition of each room, and give as many areas of the school a fresh coat of paint as possible.

Additional Notes: _____

_____

✳ *Sports Physical Examinations*

The scheduling of sports physicals for the fall season is important. Because many students go away for the summer, scheduling the physicals in June will enable all students to be eligible to participate on the first day of fall practice.

Additional Notes: _____

_____

✳ *Chairpersons' Schedules*

Keep the summer schedule of your chairpersons close at hand. They are of critical importance in responding to the many questions that may arise over the summer. Sudden retirements, concerns over a grade, and a special report requested by the superintendent are all examples of the types of issues they may develop at any time and that might call for the information provided by this schedule.

Additional Notes: _____

_____

✳ *Summer School Principal*

The summer school principal is often a teacher or assistant principal. A meeting with the summer school principal to review the operation and expectations for summer school will help to ensure a smooth program.

Additional Notes: _____

_____

✳ *Opening of School*

By now, planning should be well underway for the opening of school. Welcome-back letters, materials, and supplies should be organized and prepared. The activities calendar and a list of meetings should be prepared as well.

Additional Notes: _____

_____

June Personnel

✳ *Staff Evaluations*

All faculty and staff evaluations should be completed by the close of school. Have your secretary keep a list of all such documents, and have him or her remind you of any outstanding evaluations.

Additional Notes: _____

_____

✳ Teaching Schedules

Teachers are often anxious about their schedule for the coming year. Coordinate with the other administrators and department chairpersons to release this information to all staff members at the same time. Remember to explain that all schedules are tentative and that some changes may be necessary over the summer.

Additional Notes: _____

_____

June Checklists

June Key Tasks

Major Assignments	Date Started	Date Completed	Days on Task
Oversee the preparation of final examinations			
Issue final report cards and review final grades			
Complete all end-of-year reports			
Organize the final locker cleanout			
Conduct the graduation ceremony			
Organize the awards assembly			
Run an early registration for summer school			
Publish teacher sign-out procedures			
Attend end-of-year activities			
Submit summer work recommendations for guidance hours and curriculum writing			
Develop a list of students who have not returned books or equipment			

June Communications

	Assignment
	Provide the board of education with plans for the coming year
	Attend the PTA installation night
	Notify faculty and staff of your summer schedule
	Establish a schedule of individual faculty meetings

June Planning

	Assignment
	Develop deadlines for the submission of grades and failure lists
	Schedule chaperones for all final activities
	Meet with the head custodian to finalize the summer cleaning and painting schedule
	Schedule sports physicals
	Review all chairpersons' schedules and vacation dates
	Meet with the summer school principal
	Develop preliminary plans for opening of school

June Personnel

	Assignment
	Have your secretary check that all evaluations have been completed
	Announce next year's teaching schedules

JUNE CALENDAR

MONTH: JUNE

YEAR: _____

MONDAY	TUESDAY	WEDNESDAY	THURSDAY	FRIDAY	SATURDAY / SUNDAY

Notes: _____

Ricken, R., Simon, R., & Terc, M. The High School Principal's Calender. © 2000. Corwin Press, Inc.

Resources

Sample Documents

A. Teachers' Manual Revisions Memo
B. Teachers' Manual Index
C. Meetings Calendar Memo
D. Fundraising Calendar Memo
E. Building Security Memo
F. Orientation Agenda
G. Weekly Memo
H. National Honor Society Selection Process
I. Homecoming Parade Memo
J. Use of Building Memo
K. How to Help Memo
L. Cap and Gown Letter
M. Emergency Drills Memo
N. Class Elections Memos
O. Locker Cleanup Memos
P. End-of-Year Checkout List

Resource A
Teachers' Manual Revisions Memo

Memorandum

TO: All the Professional Staff

FROM: Principal

DATE: June

RE: Teachers' Manual Revisions

This year's teachers' manual reflected many changes in both format and content. Many hours went into making it more appealing and functional. Its primary purpose remains the same: namely, to serve as a practical guide to our new teachers and a ready reference to our veterans. Most procedures and practices that we find extant here at the high school are included in the manual.

Your input is critical for improving the manual. Along these lines, may I ask for your suggestions for improvement. Please write your suggestions on the attached page, and hand them in with your copy of the manual to the main office. Include items for addition or deletion, and feel free to inform us of mistakes of any kind, including spelling, grammar, and, most important, errors in content.

Our intention, as always, is to make our manual a document truly reflective of what actually takes place here at the high school.

The bottom line is this: If we are going to have a manual, let's make it the best we can!

Resource B
Teachers' Manual Index

Your High School Teachers' Manual Index

TOPIC	PAGE

Resource C
Meetings Calendar Memo

Memorandum

To: All Student Activities Advisors

From: Principal

Date: October

Re: Student Activities Meeting Calendar

Last year, we established a calendar to help advisors coordinate their meetings with the purpose to avoid scheduling conflicts among our clubs and organizations. The calendar seemed to work well, and several advisors have asked me to continue the practice. Therefore, please check the *Student Activities Meeting Calendar* before you schedule your next meeting. Please try to avoid conflicts, but, in any event, enter your club's meeting date and time on the calendar so that others may know your intentions. The *Student Activities Meeting Calendar* will be located in the main office.

As always, thanks for your cooperation, and have a great year with your club.

Resource D
Fundraising Calendar Memo

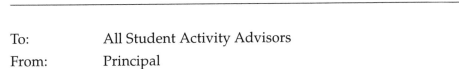

To:	All Student Activity Advisors
From:	Principal
Date:	September
Re:	Candy Sales Fundraising Calendar

Please examine the following *Candy Sales Fundraising Calendar* very carefully. If you detect a mistake or an omission, please bring it to my attention as soon as possible. If your club is listed and you decide not to use the assigned dates, kindly notify me so that I may assign your spot to another group. Finally, all groups are reminded to stay within their sales period. Have a great year!

Candy Sales Fundraising Calendar

School Week	Type of Fundraiser	Group Assigned	Assigned Calendar Dates
1 & 2	Too Early		
3	Candy Sale	S. O. Organization	_____ - _____
4	Candy Sale	Junior Class	_____ - _____
5	Candy Sale	Marching Band	_____ - _____
6	Candy Sale	Cheerleaders	_____ - _____
7	Candy Sale	Thespians	_____ - _____
8	Candy Sale	Senior Class	_____ - _____
9	Candy Sale	Chorus Concert Singers	_____ - _____
10	Candy Sale	Freshmen Class	_____ - _____

11	Candy Sale	Junior Class	_____-_____
12	Candy Sale	Dance Club	_____-_____
13	Candy Sale	Sophomore Class	_____-_____
14	Candy Sale	Freshmen Class	_____-_____

*** During Winter Regents Week, there will be no fundraising activities.

15	Candy Sale	Senior Class	_____-_____
16	Candy Sale	School Newspaper	_____-_____
17	Candy Sale	Freshmen Class	_____-_____
18	Candy Sale	Junior Class	_____-_____
19	Candy Sale	Cheerleaders	_____-_____
20	Candy Sale	Foreign Language Club	_____-_____
21	Candy Sale	Mock Trials	_____-_____
22	Candy Sale	Orchestra	_____-_____
23	Candy Sale	Freshmen Class	_____-_____
24	Candy Sale	School Newspaper	_____-_____
25	Candy Sale	Sophomore Class	_____-_____
26	Candy Sale	Portuguese Club	_____-_____
27	Candy Sale	School Newspaper	_____-_____
28	Candy Sale	National Honor Society	_____-_____
29	Candy Sale	Yearbook	_____-_____
30	Candy Sale	Yearbook	_____-_____
31	Candy Sale	Cheerleading	_____-_____
32	Candy Sale	Senior Class	_____-_____
33	Candy Sale	First Aid Club	_____-_____
34	Candy Sale	Freshmen Class	_____-_____

Resource E
Building Security Memo

Memorandum

To: All Staff
From: Principal
Date: October
Re: Building Security

The security of our school building is always a concern.

In an effort to consolidate our forces, we ask that you take the following actions:

1. When you leave your room at the end of the day, please *ensure that your windows are closed and locked.* This is a must for teachers who have classrooms located on the first floor.

2. It is a good idea to lock your room whenever you will be out for any length of time, and a must at the end of the day.

3. Teachers should place their gradebooks in a secure place. The same advice applies to pocketbooks, keys, wallets, and so forth. A locked file cabinet will go a long way toward preventing unwanted losses.

4. As you walk about the building, take note of anything suspicious that might lead to a problem. Usually, we can nip a potential problem in the bud if we get an early tip from you. Writings on a wall or marks on a door may be the early warning signs of a student in need of help. Please notify one of the administrators when something seems amiss. Do not wait until it is too late.

5. Students should not be allowed out of your class without a pass. Please limit the number of passes that you issue.

6. When you notice someone who looks as if he or she is "up to no good," notify the office immediately. Remember to take note of the time and location, and to write down as many details as soon as you can. Such details seem insignificant, but often prove to be the missing pieces to a larger picture.

In conclusion, our high school is a safe school. The *vast* majority of our students are decent and honest. They respect us as educators, and appreciate our efforts to make them better people. On the other hand, the number of disruptive students is minimal in comparison. However, since "one rotten apple can spoil the barrel," we must be ever vigilant to combat their activities. The suggestions outlined above should help to keep our school free of unnecessary acts of vandalism and preserve our well-earned reputation as a great place to be.

As always, thanks for your cooperation.

Resource F
Orientation Agenda

Principal's Orientation Presentation: To Teachers New to Our School District

The session will run for approximately one hour—from 2:20 to 3:20 p.m.

Agenda

* *Student Activities and Coaching*

Discuss the types of clubs and organizations offered at our high school.
Distribute copies of the student activities guidebook.
Discuss the hiring of advisors.
Remind them that their attendance at student events is noticed, especially by students.

* *Student Activities Participation Policy*

Discuss its overall purpose.
Discuss how it works.
Explain the teacher's role and the advisor's role.

* *Audience Control*

Discuss the overall purpose of having teachers serve as audience control monitors.
Explain how teachers are chosen to work as audience control monitors.
Discuss what constitutes appropriate supervision (distant nearness, common sense, etc.).
Remind them to exhibit professional conduct at events such as dances.

* *Grading Policies at Our High School: Frequently Asked Questions*

Gradebooks—How often should you test?

What criteria will make up a student's grade? (Remind them to inform the students of their policy in writing.)

When are grades due?

When are interims due? Who should receive an interim (bad and good)?

What are scanforms?

What are verification sheets?

How can you correct mistakes?

✻ *Miscellaneous Concerns*

Suggest that they use the buddy system their first year.

Remind them to read the teachers' manual.

Discuss discipline progression.

Discuss seating charts.

Remind them to tell classes what is expected and to be prepared to enforce their policies.

Discuss issuing passes: in school, okay under certain circumstances; out of school, not okay.

Discuss after school availability.

Discuss per period attendance.

Remind them that visitors to the classes are not permitted.

Remind them to lock doors and cabinets when they are not around.

Discuss fire drills: eight in the fall, four in the spring; bring gradebooks, lock doors, and remind students they may not smoke outside.

Remind them to keep valuables—gradebooks, keys, field trip money, wallets, pocketbooks—out of sight.

Discuss paycheck dates and procedures.

Discuss lesson plan books: Use a notebook.

Discuss teacher absences.

Discuss accident reports: Better to be safe than sorry!

Discuss emergency call box keys and their limitations.

Suggest that they take a first aid course and get certified.

Remind them that visitors to the building should have passes from the main office.

Discuss emergency windows: Keep them accessible.

Discuss eating in the classroom: Remind them that some students do not have a scheduled lunch period.

Discuss passes to the health office, to the telephone, and so forth.

Remind them to close all windows at the end of the day, especially the last teacher who uses a room.

Remind them to turn all lights out if the room will be unused the following period, and at the end of the day.

Discuss the *Initiate Custodial Work* request form.

✻ *Handouts*

Copy of the First-Quarter Grade Reporting memo.

Copy of a scanform.

Copy of the student activities guidebook.

Copy of the audience control assignment sheet for coverage of a high school event.

Resource G
Weekly Memo

Principal's Weekly Bulletin

Friday, October

1. As we enter the fifth week of school, allow me to extend a sincere thank-you for a great start of another school year. Obviously, your efforts made this possible!

2. Ideally, you will want to get some fresh air and sunshine this weekend and can attend our annual Homecoming festivities. Whether you watch the parade from Main Street or walk with the band to the football field, your presence will be greatly appreciated. Our team is currently undefeated, and they hope to be victorious in front of a large hometown crowd.

3. Thanks for your participation in last week's Open School Night. Many parents have sent complimentary letters noting the informative and friendly nature of this annual event. Evenings such as this one help our parents to see and understand what a fine and dedicated faculty you are.

4. The high school PTA provides us with a great deal of support for all we do. All of their fundraising efforts help to support our programs and our kids. Remember, the *T* in PTA is an important element in this organization, because it symbolizes the joining together of the many school constituencies. Soon, the PTA Membership Committee will be putting a reminder in your mailboxes asking you to become an active member. Let's get the number of faculty members in the 90% to 100% range! Thank you for joining.

5. We are coming up to the end of the first interim period. We request that you use the available comments broadly and provide feedback to as many parents and students as possible. Many of our parents appreciate knowing how their youngsters are doing, so try to give each student a comment or two.

6. The field trip season is upon us. Please remember to place the date of any upcoming trip on the *Field Trip Calendar* (located in the attendance office) to help us monitor the number of trips going out on any one day. Also, please do not forget the ten-day requirement for submitting the list of students going on the trip. These rules help make things go so much smoother.

Next Week's Activities of Note

Monday Oct 5 (a 5 day)   Field trip to the Museum of Modern Art, 9:00 a.m. to 2:00 p.m., Mr. Bogach's art classes

Supervisory Cabinet Meeting

Tuesday Oct 6 (a 6 day)   College Mini-Fair held in the library, 10:00 to 11:00 a.m.

Parents' Sports Club meeting, 7:30 p.m.

Teacher training course—Introduction to Word Processing, room 357

Wednesday Oct 7 (a 1 day)   Cognitive abilities testing of new entrants

New teacher orientation meeting with the principal, room 112

Thursday Oct 8 (a 2 day)   Senior class picture, period 2 in the gym

National Honor Society meeting in the auditorium, 3:00 p.m.

Board of education meeting, 8:00 p.m.

Friday Oct 9 (a 3 day)   Field trip to the County Court House, 9:00 a.m., Mr. Ross's law class

First-quarter interims are due on Monday

Resource H
National Honor Society
Selection Process

National Honor Society Selection Process

✳ *Step 1: Obtain Eligibility Lists*

Senior Candidates: In October, our records clerk will calculate the cumulative averages for all seniors. When averaging, the clerk will include all courses in which grades are given. The records clerk will submit the list of all seniors who have achieved cumulative averages of 85% or above to the Honor Society Committee advisor.

Junior Candidates: In April, our records clerk will calculate the cumulative averages for all juniors. When averaging, the clerk will include all courses in which grades are given. The records clerk will submit the list of all juniors who have achieved cumulative averages of 90% or above to the Honor Society Committee advisor.

✳ *Step 2: Applications/Activity Informational Sheets*

The Honor Society Committee advisor *will hand deliver* a copy of the application form, titled *Activity Information Sheet for National Honor Society Candidates*, to each eligible student. The form asks candidates to list evidence of their *service* and *leadership* to the school or community, as well as any involvement in sports, clubs, and other school organizations or activities for all their years in high school. The candidates will be given a deadline for returning the application if they wish to be considered for induction. Failure to submit an application will result in the withdrawal of the student's name from the eligibility list. If a student does not wish to apply, he or she will be *requested* to sign an "I do not wish to apply" statement.

The Honor Society Committee advisor *will personally contact* those who said that they wished to apply and took an application, but who failed to return the form by the deadline date. Candidates who fail to return their application after the second request will be dropped as potential candidates.

✳ *Step 3: Xerox Copies of the Applications*

Enough copies of the students' applications for all the members of the selection committee will be made to help the committee arrive at its decision.

✳ *Step 4: Criteria for Induction*

Each candidate will be judged on four areas: *scholarship, character, service,* and *leadership.*

* ✳ Scholarship will be calculated by the records clerk.

* ✳ Character will be judged by the faculty.

* ✳ Service will be judged by the selection committee.

* ✳ Leadership will be judged by the selection committee.

✳ *Step 5: Ask the Faculty to Rate the Candidates on Their Character*

Send out *Character Rating Sheets* to the entire faculty, including teachers, directors, and administrators. Request that faculty members indicate a character rating for each student they know well. These sheets should be returned to the principal's office. The Honor Society Committee advisor will average the scores, and arrive at an average character rating for each candidate. This average will be placed on the candidate's *Overall Rating Sheet,* which will be distributed to all committee members.

✳ *Step 6: Have Advisors and Coaches Rate the Candidates on Service and Leadership*

Send out *Service and Leadership Rating Sheets* to advisors and coaches listed on each candidate's informational sheet. These forms should be returned to the Honor Society Committee advisor. They will be used at the meeting of the selection committee to ascertain the feelings of the advisors and coaches who have worked closely with the candidates. This will assist the committee to arrive at an informative and appropriate rating for each candidate's service and leadership.

✳ *Step 7: Prepare Folders for Selection Committee Members*

Prepare folders, one for each selection committee member. Each folder should contain the following items:

* ✳ An outline of the selection process.

* ✳ A rating sheet containing the names of all eligible candidates.

* ✳ Selection guidelines for rating candidates.

* ✳ A copy of each candidate's *Activity Information Sheet.*

✳ *Step 8: Members Should Arrive at an Initial Rating*

Once the committee members receive their folders, each member should review the candidates' informational sheets. They should then assign each candidate a rating for service and leadership based on what the candidate has listed. Committee members may assign a rating of from 1 to 5, including half points, such as 3.5. The ratings should be placed on the *Overall Rating Sheet*. Once completed, these sheets should be submitted to the Honor Society Committee advisor. They will be listed on a *Summary Rating Sheet*, which will be distributed to all the members at the first meeting.

✳ *Step 9: Prepare the Summary Rating Sheet*

The Honor Society Committee advisor will compile the ratings of all the candidates from each committee member, and will arrive at an average number of points for each candidate. The advisor will make sufficient copies to distribute to members of the committee.

✳ *Step 10: Convene the Committee Meeting*

Hold the first meeting of the selection committee to discuss the candidates and to vote on their induction into the Honor Society.

✳ *Step 11: The Voting Process*

The committee will discuss and vote on each candidate, starting with the candidate who received the highest ranking based on the initial ratings of the committee members. The chairperson will ask if anyone would like to discuss (pro and con) the candidate being considered. When discussion comes to an end, a formal vote will be taken. The members of the committee will indicate by raising their hands if they are in favor of or against the candidate's induction into the society. A simple majority will be sufficient for induction approval. In case of a tie, the candidate will be considered rejected for induction. Any candidate who fails to be accepted on the first formal vote of the committee *may be* discussed at the end of the meeting. Any member may request that a second vote be taken. Note: The motion to have a second vote must be seconded by another member.

✳ *Step 12: Notification of Those Who Were Rejected*

The Honor Society Committee advisor *will personally inform* each candidate who failed to be inducted into the society. The advisor will notify each student as to the reason(s) for the rejection and will advise each of his or her right to an appeal.

✳ *Step 13: Announcement of Those Who Were Selected*

After all the candidates who failed to be inducted have been notified, then—and only then—will the names of those who were chosen be announced over the PA system.

✳ *Step 14: The Appeal Process*

All candidates who failed to be accepted for induction will have the right to appeal the decision to the principal.

✳ *Step 15: Official Notification and Pictures*

Each student chosen will be sent a congratulatory letter signed by the principal. Recently chosen candidates will have their picture taken, and it will be placed in the local papers.

Resource I
Homecoming Parade Memo

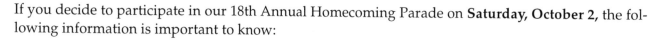

Memorandum

To: All Homecoming Day Participants
From: Homecoming Committee Chairperson
Date: October
Re: Homecoming Parade

If you decide to participate in our 18th Annual Homecoming Parade on **Saturday, October 2,** the following information is important to know:

1. All participants are to assemble at 11:30 a.m. on Abby Road, south of Main Street. Cars and floats should arrive at 11:15 a.m. Groups that decide to participate will receive the official "Order of the March" when they arrive. See the parade coordinator for specifics.
   NOTE: The streets for assembling will be blocked off to normal traffic.

2. Groups should assemble in lines of approximately six across. Once your group steps out onto Main Street, please arrange your members to the width of the street assigned for our use.

3. The parade will commence shortly after 12:00 noon.

4. The parade route will proceed east on Main Street directly to the football stadium. The parade will then continue around the track of the field. The floats will park at the east end of the field after traveling around the track. If your float will not be parking, please exit the stadium through the southeast gate near the Booster Club concession stand. Marchers will continue past the visitors' bleachers to end at the west end of the stadium. Please ask your group not to disassemble until this time.

5. In case of rain, the parade may have to be canceled. The rain date is **Saturday, October 23.** If in doubt, call the high school main office: You may hear a recorded message. *Do not* call before 10:30 a.m.

6. All organizations must carry a banner displaying their group's name.

7. Selling along the parade route is prohibited.

8. The high school administration and the board of education respectfully request that no political activity or campaigning of any type be undertaken by marchers in the high school Homecoming Parade.

Pre-game ceremonies will commence at the conclusion of the parade. The football game is scheduled to start promptly at 2:00 p.m.

Any questions regarding the parade should be directed to the principal's office.

Resource J
Use of Building Memo

Memorandum

To: All Staff

From: Principal/Head Custodian

Date: September

Re: Use of the building on weekends and holidays

Staff members who plan to enter the school building when the general school population is not in attendance are requested to report directly to the head custodian's office (room 152) when they first enter the building on such days. They should indicate their presence in the building by placing their name and the time they entered on a special sign-in sheet, which will be located by the doorway to the office. By signing in, you will be alerting the custodian on duty of your presence, and, by indicating the length of time you expect to be in the building, you will help to prevent security alarms from being set off accidentally. On the sign-in sheet, kindly indicate the location where you will be working. By indicating your location, you will be assisting the custodial staff in their efforts to promote a safe environment. Furthermore, if you are unsure if the building is going to be open on a particular day, check with the main office. This applies especially to days that might fall during a vacation.

Whenever possible, please notify the head custodian of your intentions at least two days before you actually expect to come in. For security reasons, our custodians often keep the exterior doors locked on weekends, although they may be working in the building. Prior notification would help to expedite your admittance into the building.

Remember, our goal is to keep you and the building safe and sound.

On the reverse side of this memo, you will find a copy of the sign-in sheet referred to in the above statement.

Your cooperation in this matter will be greatly appreciated.

Resource K
How to Help Memo

Memorandum

To: Parents of 8th-Grade Students

From: Principal

Date: December

Re: How to help your 9th-grade student succeed at our high school

Parents often ask, "How do so many kids get on the honor roll? What is their secret?"

I don't believe there is one secret to their success. Kids who do well in school do many things that bring them success. Here are some of the things that those who succeed adhere to:

1. Those who succeed work hard. Usually, the harder they work the better they do! They put in hours of study and practice at whatever they wish to do well. Don't deceive yourself: Natural ability is nice, but the secret of the champions is that practice pays off. *Practice, practice, practice.*

2. Those who succeed *have a goal.* They have the courage to say, "No, I have to study," when they must.

3. Those who succeed *are well organized.*

4. Those who succeed participate in class. They take notes, *ask questions,* and exchange ideas.

5. Those who succeed apply themselves at home. They take their homework seriously, and realize that the time spent in class is *only a part* of the learning process.

6. Those who succeed study their notes on a regular basis and prepare for exams a few days in advance of the test. Cramming is a last resort! Follow the *PQRST* (*Preview, Question, Read, Study, Test*) system whenever possible.

7. Those who succeed have an optimistic outlook on life. For them, *the glass is half full* rather than half empty.

8. Those who succeed *come to class prepared* to work, with pen, paper, and notebook.

9. Those who succeed try to *manage their time*. They maintain a balance between their outside interests and their school responsibilities. They set up a schedule and follow it.

10. Those who succeed make every effort to complete their assignments. They set aside time to *do their homework assignments* on a regular basis.

11. Those who succeed *seek help* when they feel they have to. They are not afraid to admit they need assistance.

12. Those who succeed make a conscious effort to *learn the vocabulary* of the subject. There are such things as math dictionaries, for example.

13. Those who succeed have learned that *for every effect there is a cause*. Once this basic truth is embraced, students realize that life depends more on hard work than luck and the breaks!

14. Those who succeed are usually involved with or engaged in some worthwhile activity.

You might be asking, "What can we as parents do to help?"
Here are some suggestions:

1. Realize that your children experience *tremendous peer pressure*, either real or imaginary. Be understanding.

2. Realize that they may be *very self-conscious* about themselves. Adolescence is a difficult stage to get through for many. Remember, no two youngsters go through the stages at the same time; their reactions to each stage may be totally different from their sister's or brother's reaction. We are the same in many ways, yet different in others.

3. Help your children develop their expectations, but *know when to back off*.

4. Help your children solve life's problems. As they get older, *be a safety net*! They must learn how to fly, but don't let them crash.

5. Remember that your personal lifestyle and actions will always speak louder than words.

6. Try to *be flexible* when appropriate. Roll with the punches.

7. Talk to your youngsters: You never know when you will get through. Try to see the world through their perspective. *Be as understanding as possible.*

8. Exercise great patience! The pressures of life are sometimes great, but *remember that you are the adult*. Try your best not to act like a kid, especially when the tensions get high.

9. *Talk to other parents.* You will be shocked to learn that they are experiencing many of the same things as you. And don't forget to talk to those who have gone through it already; they often have some great insights.

10. *Don't give up* your role as a parent. You will always have an influence in your youngster's life, even if you think no one is paying attention.

11. Parents must *persevere.* Follow the example of the turtle: Be slow, patient, and use your hard shell sometimes.

12. Try to *out-fox them.* Different approaches work better with different kids. Love, reason, reward, threaten, withhold, reciprocate: Use your imagination! Be resourceful.

13. Remember, *there is life after raising children.* Guard against the divide-and-conquer routine so often used on parents.

14. Maintain your sense of humor. *Maintain a sense of balance!* Enjoy your children as much as possible.

If we work together, all our students can succeed.

Resource L
Cap and Gown Letter

Your High School   **School Street**
Your Town, State, Zip Code

Principal
Assistant Principal

February

Dear Parent or Guardian:

Although graduation is still months away, it is time to begin planning now. This year's commencement will be held at 10:00 a.m. on Saturday, June 24, at Center Auditorium. As you know, it is traditional for our high school graduates to wear caps and gowns at their commencement exercises.

On Thursday, February 24, a representative of the National Cap and Gown Company will be at our high school to take orders for graduation caps and gowns. The representative will be taking orders in Room 112, from 10:15 a.m. to 1:00 p.m.

This is the only time the representatives will be at the school, so it is essential that your son or daughter order his or her cap and gown on this date. The rental fee is $16.00 and is payable at the time the order is placed. Checks or money orders should be made out to "National Cap and Gown Company." (Cash will be accepted.)

Since only those graduating seniors who have ordered caps and gowns will be permitted to participate in the graduation ceremony, I would appreciate your telling your senior that it is important to get his or her order in on Thursday, February 24.

Sincerely yours,

Principal

P.S.   ***Extras***
The rental fee includes a souvenir cap and tassel. Additional tassels may be purchased for $4.00 each. Souvenir Mega-Tassels may be purchased for $5.00 each. Souvenir Mini-Tassel Key Rings may be purchased for $4.00 each.

A late fee of $5.00 will be charged to all students who order their cap and gown after Thursday, February 24.

Resource M
Emergency Drills Memo

Memorandum

To:	All Staff
From:	Principal
Date:	February
Re:	Emergency Drills
	Shelter Drill & Go Home: Friday, March 17

On **Friday, March 17,** our school district will be dismissing all students approximately 25 minutes earlier than usual. All state school districts are now required by state law to conduct two emergency drills: a *Shelter Drill* and a *Go Home Drill*. A formal announcement will be made over the PA system directing all classes to report to either the auditorium or the gymnasium under the direction of their classroom teacher. Students should bring their belongings to the shelter area; they will not be returning to their classrooms. After everyone is assembled in their assigned shelter areas, we will make a short address and dismiss the groups from these locations with instructions to exit the building immediately after they retrieve their books and coats from their lockers. We will be using the following modified bell schedule during the day:

Modified Bell Schedule

Period 1	7:37-8:14	(37 min.)
Period 2	8:18-9:00	(42 min.)
Period 3	9:04-9:41	(37 min.)
Period 4	9:45-10:22	(37 min.)
Period 5	10:26-11:02	(36 min.)
Period 6	11:06-11:42	(36 min.)
Period 7	11:46-12:23	(37 min.)
Period 8	12:27-1:04	(37 min.)
Period 9	1:08-1:45	(37 min.)

* *Please Note:*

Classes located on the third floor will be asked to report to the gymnasium. Teachers on the third floor are asked to use the stairwells nearest to the back of the building.

Classes located on the first and second floors will be asked to report to the auditorium. Teachers on the second floors are asked to use the stairwells nearest to the front of the building.

* *Please Note:*

All after-school activities and meetings are cancelled. This applies to students who take the bus or walk to school.

There will be no late bus.

Teachers are reminded to bring their class rosters with them.

Resource N
Class Elections Memos

Memorandum

To:	All Staff
From:	Principal and Class Advisors
Date:	April
Re:	Election of Class Officers on May 6

In the very near future, we will be holding our annual class officer elections. This year's class advisors will be asking for candidates from each of the grade levels via the Morning News Reports. Experienced teachers and our newer staff members should, I hope, find the following schedule and election procedures to be informative. Student elections provide our youngsters an opportunity to participate in one of America's greatest offerings: namely, the right to choose their own leaders. This privilege is one of the cornerstones of our nation's democratic process. We hope many fine candidates will step forward and place their names in contention for an office. Win or lose, most will learn invaluable lessons about the process as well as themselves. Please encourage your students to get involved!

Schedule for Class Elections

Monday-Friday	April 19-23	A call for candidates
Friday	April 23	Candidates' petitions are due by 3 p.m.
Wednesday-Thursday	April 28-May 6	Poster campaign days
Thursday	May 6	Candidates' speeches shown in social studies classes
Thursday	May 6	Election say in social studies classes (using paper ballots)

✳ *Faculty Involvement*

Teachers of all potential candidates are asked to verify that the candidates have achieved an overall average of 75% or higher for *the first three quarters* in their particular subject. Teachers should sign the candidates' petitions indicating this fact. If the candidates' average is lower than 75%, the teacher should indicate that fact. Candidates who have two or more averages below 75% will not be permitted to run for a class office. Students who are failing one or more subjects will not be permitted to run for a class office as well.

✳ *Regulations*

✳ Each candidate must meet all academic and behavioral standards.

✳ Each candidate must secure 24 endorsements from students in his or her own grade level.

✳ Each candidate must secure verification of his or her grade average from all teachers in the subjects in which he or she is currently enrolled.

✳ All petitions must be submitted no later than **3:00 p.m., Friday, April 23.**

✳ All campaign posters must be approved by the main office.

✳ Each candidate may place:

4 posters on each floor

1 poster in the cafeteria

1 poster in the lobby

✳ Any other type of campaign literature must be approved in advance by the principal.

Memorandum

To: All Class Advisors

From: Principal

Date: April

Re: Class Elections—Reminders

Once you receive the candidates' petitions, please keep in mind the following procedures:

1. Forward the petitions to the principal's secretary so that they can be kept on file in the main office.

2. Please monitor the poster situation. If a candidate is running unopposed, he or she should still make posters and prepare a brief statement about goals and expectations. All materials, including flyers and handouts, that are distributed on behalf of any candidate must be approved by the main office. Breaking of this rule may result in a candidate's disqualification.

3. Please arrange with our TV technician to have the candidates' speeches taped. Once a taping time is agreed upon, *kindly notify teachers of each candidate in writing* to avoid unnecessary conflicts. Try your best to conduct the taping during a free period whenever possible.

4. The television presentations and the actual vote are set for **Thursday, May 6.** The speeches will be shown during our regular social studies classes. Social studies teachers will receive a separate memo outlining their election responsibilities.

5. Following the viewing of the candidates' speeches, the election will take place in the social studies classes. Advisors are asked to help prepare the election ballot by submitting the names of all candidates running for office and the office for which they are running. The main office will prepare the actual ballot, and will then make enough copies for each class and distribute sufficient ballots to each social studies teacher.

6. Social studies teachers should collect all the ballots, and should place them in the envelopes provided. The envelopes will be picked up during the day or handed in to the main office personally by the teacher. *Do not entrust a student to hand the ballots in.* Social studies teachers should be encouraged to limit the number of ballots that are being handed out. This will, we hope, help to prevent ballot stuffing.

7. The actual counting of ballots will be done in the principal's office with the help of our student organization officers. Advisors will be notified of the results as soon as they are available. The names of those elected will be announced over the PA system or during the student organization assembly. Those who previously held an office, but were not elected, will be notified prior to the actual announcement.

8. If no student in a particular office receives a majority of the votes cast, there will be a special runoff election between the top two vote-getters.

Memorandum

To: All Candidates
From: Principal and Class Advisors
Date: April
Re: Class Elections—Procedures

Schedule for Class Elections

Monday-Friday	April 19-23	A call for candidates
Friday	April 23	Candidates' petitions are due by 3 p.m.
Wednesday-Thursday	April 28-May 6	Poster campaign days
Thursday	May 6	Candidates' speeches shown in social studies classes
Thursday	May 6	Election day in social studies classes (using paper ballots)

✷ Regulations

* Each candidate must meet all academic and behavioral standards, which include that all potential candidates achieve an overall average of at least 75% for *the first three quarters* in every subject in which they are enrolled. Teachers should sign the candidate's petition indicating this fact. If the candidate's average is lower than 75%, the teacher should indicate that fact. Candidates who have two or more averages below 75% will not be permitted to run for a class office. Students who are failing one or more subjects will not be permitted to run for a class office as well.

* Each candidate must secure 24 endorsements from students in his or her own grade level.

* Each candidate must secure grade verifications from all their current teachers.

* All petitions must be submitted no later than **3 p.m., Friday, April 23.**

* All campaign posters must be approved by the principal.

* Each candidate may place at most:

     4 posters on each floor

     1 poster in the cafeteria

     1 poster in the lobby

* All campaign-related literature must be approved by the principal prior to distribution.

* Violations of any of the above rules may result in the candidate's disqualification.

✳ *Additional Items*

The class advisor will submit the names of all candidates to the main office along with their petitions. The class advisor will also help to prepare an election ballot. The main office will distribute enough official ballots and envelopes to each social studies teacher.

On **Thursday, May 6,** social studies teachers will allow their students the opportunity to view the candidates' speeches. Following the speeches, they will conduct the election in their respective classrooms. After each student has had a chance to vote, ballots will be collected and placed in the election envelope.

The main office will collect the ballots from each social studies teacher. All votes will be tabulated at that time, and the results will be announced via the PA system. In the event that no candidate receives a clear majority of the votes in the general election, a special runoff election will be held between the top two vote-getters.

Thanks for your cooperation, and good luck!

Resource O
Locker Cleanup Memos

Memorandum

To: All Staff
From: Principal
Date: June
Re: Locker Cleanup

The following memo outlines the procedures we will be using here at the high school to clean out all student lockers and to relock them for the summer months.

1. On the last day of school, we will conduct a schoolwide locker cleanup during period 2. Garbage pails and bins will be placed in all hallways for students to discard items that are no longer needed.

2. Locker cleanup day will be announced to all students over the PA system and through an official notice that will be distributed to all students prior to the actual cleanup date.

3. At the end of the school day, students will be requested to remove all items from their lockers, to remove their locks from the locking mechanism, and to lock it to the handle just above the locking hole. This will allow our custodians to enter the locker to disinfect and make any necessary adjustments.

4. Two student summer office workers will then open any locks that are still in the locking hole, and will remove all items from those lockers. They will place all valuables in a plastic bag, and place the locker number and student's name on the bag for future reference.

5. Any textbooks or library books found in the lockers will be returned to the appropriate departments or the library.

6. After the summer workers have completed their final cleanup, the custodial staff will check each locker and make repairs as needed. Once this is completed, the student workers will relock (using the locking hole) all lockers, will put different locks on the senior lockers, and will record these changes in the locker book.

Everything outlined above will hopefully go smoothly!

If you have any questions, please contact my office. As always, thanks for your help.

To All Students

Locker Cleanup Day

Locker cleanup day is scheduled to take place during homeroom on the last day of classes, **Tuesday, June 3.**

Please follow the procedures listed below:

* All students are asked to throw out any items that they will no longer need. Garbage bins will be located in the hallways for your use.

* You may keep all other items in your locker until the end of the school day.

* At the end of the day, you must remove all items from your locker, remove the lock from the locking hole, and lock it on the handle just above the hole. This will keep your lock safe until next year, yet will give our custodial staff access to clean your locker and fix any mechanical parts that might not be working properly.

Seniors should follow the same procedure. Staff members from the main office will collect their locks, and seniors will be credited for returning their locks if they lock them on the handle. Seniors who fail to lock their locks on the handle will be charged $4 to replace the lock they were issued when they first came to our high school.

Good luck on your finals!

Resource P
End-of-Year Checkout List

End-of-Year Checkout List

Your High School

JUNE

Note: Please write *N/A* where an item is not applicable.

Teacher:_____

ITEM	REQUIRED INITIALS
Bulletin boards cleared, and classroom prepared for the summer.	_____ Department Director
Final examinations rated, arranged, and filed.	_____ Department Director
All failure slips submitted.	_____ Department Director
Report card scanforms completed and submitted.	_____ Department Director
Report Card Verification forms completed and submitted.	_____ Department Director
Requisitions submitted.	_____ Department Director
Book inventory submitted.	_____ Department Director
Rebind list submitted.	_____ Department Director

Science lab books and folders completed for science courses.

_____
Department Director

Examination grades submitted.

_____
Department Director

Regents report submitted.

_____
Department Director

Senior lounge key returned.

_____
Department Director

Gradebook, including the teacher's name on cover, submitted.

_____
Department Director

****

Summer Address_____

Summer Phone_____

Central treasury accounts closed (if applicable).

_____
Accounts Clerk

All keys labeled and returned (for retirees only).

_____
Head Custodian

Teacher manual returned to main office.

_____
Principal's Secretary

Final check by principal.

_____
Principal

CORWIN
PRESS

The Corwin Press logo—a raven striding across an open book—represents the happy union of courage and learning. We are a professional-level publisher of books and journals for K-12 educators, and we are committed to creating and providing resources that embody these qualities. Corwin's motto is "Success for All Learners."